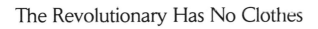

The Revolutionary Has No Clothes

The Revolutionary
Has No Clothes

Hugo Chávez's Bolivarian Farce

A. C. Clark

ENCOUNTER BOOKS
NEW YORK · LONDON

First American edition published in 2009 by Encounter Books, an activity of Encounter for Culture and Education, Inc., a nonprofit, tax exempt corporation. Encounter Books website address: www.encounterbooks.com

Manufactured in the United States and printed on acid-free paper. The paper used in this publication meets the minimum requirements of ANSI/NISO Z39.48 1992 (R 1997) (*Permanence of Paper*).

FIRST AMERICAN EDITION

LIBRARY OF CONGRESS CATALOGING-IN-PUBLICATION DATA

Clark, A. C.
    The revolutionary has no clothes : Hugo Chávez's Bolivarian farce / A.C. Clark.
        p.   cm.
    Includes index.
    ISBN-13: 978-1-59403-259-2 (hardcover : alk. paper)
    ISBN-10: 1-59403-259-9 (hardcover : alk. paper)
    1. Venezuela—Politics and government—1999–   2. Venezuela—Foreign relations—1999–   3. Venezuela—History.   4. Chávez Frías, Hugo.
    5. Authoritarianism—Venezuela.   I. Title.
    F2329.C63 2009
    987.06'42092—dc22
                                                                2009018112

10 9 8 7 6 5 4 3 2 1

CONTENTS

INTRODUCTION

W hat most non-Venezuelans know about Venezuela is that it has oil—enormous quantities of it. Indeed, Venezuela's location has made it a rather convenient supplier of oil to the United States. Venezuela's capital, Caracas, is closer to Washington, D.C. (about 2,000 miles) than it is to São Paulo, in neighboring Brazil (about 2,700 miles). By plane, the trip from Caracas to Miami is a mere two and half hours. Aside from the fact that it has oil, however, little else is widely known about Venezuela. Outsiders' knowledge is typically limited to trivia: Venezuela's infatuation with beauty pageants and plastic surgery, or the country's once popular soap operas.

During the forty or so years that preceded Hugo Chávez's seizing of power, Venezuela was markedly not newsworthy. It had by far the most stable democracy in Latin America—at times, the only real democracy in the region. Thanks above all to its immense oil revenues, Venezuela boasted the region's fastest-growing economy and highest standard of living. Thus it was a haven for all sorts of immigrants: not only economic immigrants, such as the scores of Italians, Portuguese, and Spaniards who left their ravaged European homelands in search of a livelihood, but also political immigrants, such as the many Chileans, Argentineans, and Uruguayans who fled the repressive, dictatorial regimes that proliferated in South America's southern nations in the

1970s. All these immigrants found a welcoming home in Venezuela, where they enjoyed a new prosperity and freedom from persecution.

After Chávez seized power in 1999, however, things changed dramatically. Venezuela can hardly be seen as a democracy any longer, and instead of attracting immigrants, it is losing its own citizens. On the other hand, Chávez's Venezuela is now frequently in the news and is the subject of many book-length studies, and the vast majority of contemporary references to Venezuela and to Chávez's rule are laudatory. The regime has spawned a veritable cottage industry of apologetics and panegyrics. This book seeks to correct the skewed take on Hugo Chávez and the "Bolivarian Revolution" in Venezuela.

Because Chávez has dubbed his so-called revolution "Bolivarian" in honor of Venezuela's founding father, Simón Bolívar, I shall pay special attention in the first chapter to Bolívar and his relationship to Chávez. As we shall see, Chávez often misunderstands and misquotes Bolívar, just as he regularly misinterprets and falsifies Venezuelan history. By and large, Chávez's panegyrists ignore Venezuelan history, and when they do refer to it, their main source (when not their only source) is Chávez himself. In contrast, this book draws from a variety of sources in an effort to look at Venezuelan history objectively. A passing acquaintance with this history is helpful for understanding the contemporary Venezuelan reality and grasping how it was possible for Chávez to take power and cling to it far beyond the term to which he was elected in the first place.

Chapter Two presents a biographical sketch of Hugo Chávez, with emphasis on the two most important facts lost in the panegyrists' shuffle: that Chávez has dismantled democracy in Venezuela and that his Bolivarian Revolution is a scandalous failure. Whatever progress Venezuelans had, with much effort, achieved in civilized political life during the second half of the twentieth century Chávez has effectively obliterated. Far from being a revolutionary champion of freedom, he is a stereotypical third-world buffoon. If the word "buffoon" sounds too irreverent or extreme, I beg my readers to suspend judgment until they have finished this book.

The third and final chapter examines the grotesqueness of the panegyrists' support for Chávez. Here I discuss in detail the unwarranted and unrestrained admiration that many people, from Sean Penn to Noam Chomsky, feel for Chávez. Second, this chapter addresses the fact that Chávez, unlike many other famous buffoons, is a very dangerous man. He has both the desire and the means to carry out his bellicose ambitions well beyond Venezuela's borders. Chávez has repeatedly claimed that the United States is "the most evil regime that has ever existed" and the natural enemy of any decent human being. Moreover, he has spent billions of dollars on weapons "to be used in the impending 'asymmetrical war' against the United States" and has strengthened ties with rogue regimes and terrorist groups all around the world. Surely these facts are not to be taken lightly or as *mere* buffoonery.

Perhaps the greatest difficulty in writing this book was selecting from among the myriad offensive or dangerous things that Chávez has said and done. Hardly a day goes by when Chávez is not in the news for some outrageous pronouncement. Moreover, he is his own greatest enthusiast, an inexhaustible PR mouthpiece for his own ideas and plans. The Internet has allowed me to take full advantage of Chávez's verbal incontinence. Thus, when I report that Chávez described a bout with diarrhea on national television, or asserted that gigantic camels live in the jungle, or when I say that he indeed pays homage to terrorists, I provide Internet links to footage of Chávez saying and doing these things. Actually seeing him perform is more powerful (and more sickening, I am afraid) than simply reading about it.

For reasons that will become painfully obvious, I have chosen to author this book under a pseudonym in order to protect myself and my loved ones. The facts and arguments presented here do not depend on my identity.

The Revolutionary Has No Clothes

CHAPTER ONE

VENEZUELA AND ITS HISTORY

M ost entries in the burgeoning genre of books and pamphlets on Chávez's so-called "Bolivarian Revolution" conspicuously ignore Venezuelan history, particularly the time prior to Chavez's birth.[1] But some historical background is sorely needed, in order to reveal that Chávez's ascent to power would have been impossible without Venezuela's peculiar type of political and historical myopia. A look at history will also suggest the reasons why Chávez still enjoys support among some Venezuelans, for he has effectively tapped into the mythologizing of history to which, I will argue, Venezuelans are so prone. I wish to highlight some historical events and trends of special importance to understanding Chávez and his regime.

The Colonial Period and the Founding Fathers

Venezuela was not a very important post for Spain during the colonial period, even though among Spain's mainland colonies it was the closest to Europe.[2] Today, Venezuela is the only Spanish-speaking South American country located entirely north of the equator; the other countries lying north of the equator are three smallish enclaves:

Guyana, Suriname, and French Guiana. In the colonial era, Venezuela was dwarfed by the two main Spanish viceroyalties, present-day Mexico and present-day Peru, and it was in these regions where the Spaniards found more gold and other mineral resources. Off the eastern coast of mainland Venezuela, the Spaniards exploited the pearls around Margarita Island, but this was a much smaller-scale enterprise.

Venezuela was, however, one of several supposed locations of El Dorado, the fabled city of gold. The legend gave rise to many an expedition into Venezuela's dense and dangerous jungles—from the Bavarian Ambrosius Ehinger, the first colonial governor of modern-day Venezuela in 1528,[3] to Sir Walter Raleigh in 1595, and many others between and after them. The fabulous golden city was, needless to say, never located. But the discovery of immense oil reserves in Venezuela during the early twentieth century can be seen as a roundabout confirmation of the legend.

Mexico and Peru were the centers of the most important and advanced pre-Columbian cultures: the Aztecs and the Mayans in Mexico, and the Incas in Peru. It was in Mexico and Peru that the Spanish alliances with indigenous groups proved most successful. The fact that these groups had been brutally subjugated by other indigenous peoples helps explain why they allied themselves with the Spaniards. In the regions corresponding to modern-day Venezuela, however, the alliances were not so numerous, nor were they as profitable to the Spaniards; many of the indigenous groups in Venezuela, such as the Caribs, fought the Spaniards to the death. Rather than surrender to the Spaniards once they had surrounded his hut and set it on fire, Venezuela's most celebrated indigenous leader, the chieftain Guaicaipuro (ca. 1530–1568), stormed out and accused the attackers of cowardice for trying to kill him by fire, not by the sword. He died fighting them, spear in hand.[4]

This indomitable fighting spirit has been something of a constant in Venezuelan history. It may explain, in part, the odd fact that it was in Venezuela, and not in the urban centers of Mexico or Peru, that the campaign for Latin American independence from Spain began. Mariano Picón Salas, one of Venezuela's most respected historians, once sensibly asked: "Why was it not from the great and golden viceroyalties of Peru and Mexico that the insurgent movement in Spanish America began to spread, and why did it rather spread from those provinces which in relation to economic life and colonial splendor were somewhat marginalized, like Caracas?"[5] I do not mean to suggest that the spirit exemplified by Guaicaipuro provides the full answer to this question, nor would I deny that his story has been dramatically mythologized, but it may provide a partial answer. Furthermore, and most emphatically, I do not wish to imply that such a fighting temperament was always a good thing. Venezuelans' pronounced tendency toward violence may partly explain the country's turbulent history.

One fact remains uncontested: Against all odds, it was Caracas, the capital city of this rather humble region called Venezuela—"part plantation, part ranch, and part commercial market,"[6] with a population under 40,000—that became the epicenter of the Latin American independence movement. It was in Caracas, too, where three colossal figures of the independence period were born: Francisco de Miranda (1750–1816), Andrés Bello (1781–1865), and Simón Bolívar (1783–1830).

Miranda is known as both "the Precursor" of independence and "the First Universal Venezuelan." His personal diaries, which he titled *Colombeia,* span sixty-three volumes.[7] And Miranda had much to tell indeed. From 1783 to 1784 he lived in the United States, where he befriended George Washington, Samuel Adams, and Alexander Hamilton, among others. Then he traveled widely in Europe and beyond, befriending Catherine the Great in Russia, meeting with Napoleon in Paris, and making the acquaintance of many other dignitaries. Miranda's heroism in the battlefield during the French Revolution earned him the titles of Marshall and Hero, in addition to an engraving on Paris's Arc de Triomphe. Returning home from Europe via the United States in 1805, he met with Thomas Jefferson and James Madison.

Back in Venezuela, Miranda immersed himself in the struggle for independence, which Venezuela announced for the first time on July 5, 1811. The ebb and flow of the fighting against the Spaniards—in particular, Bolívar's loss of Puerto Cabello—led Miranda to capitulate to the Royalist leader Domingo de Monteverde. Many Venezuelan insurgents criticized his surrender, and soon Miranda found himself out of favor with his former comrades. On July 31, 1812, a group of Venezuelans, Bolívar among them, arrested him, and he spent the rest of his life in various prisons. Death found Miranda in "La Carraca," a prison within a garrison in Cádiz, Spain.

Upon his arrest in 1812, Miranda is said to have expressed his disillusionment with Venezuelan politics in one of the most famous phrases in the country's lore: *"Bochinche ... puro bochinche."* Loosely translated, this means: "A farcical mess—the whole thing is just a farcical mess." These words, as will become clear, were a depressingly prescient description of Venezuelan politics to come. Indeed, Miranda's words have never been as accurate as they are now, during Chávez's regime.

Like Miranda, Andrés Bello was an impressive character, one of the most accomplished thinkers of the nineteenth century—arguably *the* most important Latin American thinker. He was, moreover, a private tutor to Bolívar, teaching him geography and literature. Bello's *Obras Completas* take up twenty-six volumes.[8] His *Civil Code* for Chile, his *Principles of International Law,* and his *Grammar of the Spanish Language* were first in their respective fields in Latin America, setting the standards by which new contributions would be measured. The most famous biography of Bello is titled *Andrés Bello: Philosopher, Poet, Philologist, Educator, Jurist, Statesman,*[9] and all these titles are well deserved. Like Miranda, Bello had a remarkable circle of acquaintances: he met Alexander von Humboldt and Aimé Bonpland during the naturalists' travels in Venezuela; during his nineteen years in London (1810–1829) he befriended his compatriot Miranda, as well as Jeremy Bentham, James Mill, and other influential British intellectuals. After London, Bello spent thirty-six years in Santiago, Chile, the city in which he died.

The fact that Miranda and Bello and many other illustrious Venezuelans, including Bolívar himself, died far away from their homeland, and that Venezuela's list of dictators seems endless, inspired one of the country's most important poets, Andrés Eloy Blanco, to lament that in Venezuela, *"el hijo vil se le eterniza adentro y el hijo grande se le muere afuera"*—"Venezuela's vile sons eternally rule it, and its noble sons die far away."[10]

Bolívar and His Misappropriation

Simón Bolívar too died abroad, rejected not only by his former comrades, but also by the population at large. While Bolívar's accomplishments were not necessarily more important than Miranda's or Bello's, he is the central figure in my sketch of Venezuelan history, given Chávez's monomaniacal obsession with Bolívar and things Bolivarian.

Shortly after taking power, Chávez bulldozed ahead with his plan to change Venezuela's official name. In 1999, merely as a result of Chávez's whim, the Republic of Venezuela officially became the "Bolivarian Republic of Venezuela." The official name of Chávez's so-called revolution is the Bolivarian Revolution. There were Bolivarian references in the names of most of the insurrectional, underground groups that Chávez created while a member of the Venezuelan Armed Forces, which themselves are now called, by Chávez's decree, the Venezuelan Bolivarian Armed Forces. And so on, *ad nauseam*.

Chávez is by no means the only Venezuelan afflicted with this Bolivarian obsession; most Venezuelans are, and have been ever since the country came into existence. The currency is called the bolívar; every Venezuelan town *has* to have a Plaza Bolívar; and so forth. The entry in the prestigious *Diccionario de Historia de Venezuela* for "Bolívar, Simón," written by Arturo Uslar Pietri, the most important Venezuelan public intellectual of the second half of the twentieth century, begins: "Towering and incomparable figure in the history of America, who had the privilege of possessing in their highest degree the gifts of the man of action and of the thinker."[11] (Such over-the-top fawning was not typical for Uslar Pietri, who tended to show more equanimity on other subjects.) Long before Chávez, Venezuelan history was replete with hagiographies of Bolívar, which surely were significant in shaping Chávez's worldview.

The books on Venezuelan history by J. L. Salcedo Bastardo, which were often required reading in Venezuelan middle schools and high schools, are good examples of the adulation of Bolívar. In the misleadingly titled *Vision and Revision of Bolívar* (where no revision of anything whatsoever goes on), Salcedo Bastardo asserts that "a remarkable aspect of the intellectual facet of the Liberator is his objectivity."[12] Elsewhere we read that "seen from a moral point of view the Liberator comes across as an enthusiastic appreciator of virtue."[13] Salcedo Bastardo also informs us that "Bolívar is above all things a politician who creates, a leader of peoples; he is the supreme interpreter of the supreme collective aspiration; a maker."[14]

To be sure, there has been a discernible countercurrent in Venezuelan historiography, an attempt to shake off the Bolivarian obsession. A good example is José Rafael Pocaterra's work, particularly his *Memorias de un Venezolano de la Decadencia,* in which he bemoans the Bolivarian verbiage afflicting his country.[15] Pocaterra suggests that it utterly distorts Bolívar the man and his deeds, and that it stands in the way of progress. Some recent thinkers have sought not merely to indict but also to diagnose and treat the Bolivarian fetish of so many Venezuelans. Notable among them are Germán Carrera Damas, who spoke of "the Bolívar cult," and Luis Castro Leiva, who coined the no less felicitous "Bolivarian theology."[16] In spite of these efforts, however, the Bolívar cult is alive and well in Venezuela.

What sets Chávez apart from the overwhelming majority of devout Bolivarians is the extent to which he mischaracterizes Bolívar. Needless to say, Chávez has found in ordinary Venezuelans a receptive audience for his spurious Bolívar, but his exploitation of Bolívar is impressive even by Venezuelan standards. He presents himself as Bolívar reincarnated;

yet the Chávez-as-Bolívar fantasy is a real farce.[17] There are important differences between the two men, and Chávez seems closest to Bolívar precisely in those aspects of Bolívar's thought which were already anachronistic and problematic in the nineteenth century.

Bolívar was an interesting figure, to be sure. He is of course well known as "El Libertador," the liberator not only of Venezuela, but also of the territories that now comprise Colombia, Ecuador, Bolivia, Panama, and Peru (where he shares the honors with San Martín). Bolívar was born into great wealth: both his paternal and his maternal genealogical lines belonged to the absolute upper crust of Venezuelan society. Both are clearly traceable back to European nobility, and both were unmistakably white, at a time when whiteness did play a role in Venezuelan society and politics.[18]

Bolívar became an orphan at a very early age, losing his father by the time he was three years old and his mother when he was nine. He was reared by a host of relatives and by two black slaves, Hipólita and Matea. Chávez has sought to portray Bolívar as a symbol of racial freedom and equality based on the fact that he loved these slaves very much, Hipólita above all. But Chávez has hardly presented any evidence of heightened racial tolerance on Bolívar's part beyond the rather unexceptional fact that he was fond of his nannies. In any case, Chávez has exalted Negra Matea and Negra Hipólita to the status of national heroines, in an obviously exploitive way, and there currently are plans to exhume their bodies and bring them to the National Pantheon.[19]

In fact, Chávez has a particular interest in digging up corpses. On December 17, 2007, during a speech commemorating the anniversary of Bolívar's death, Chávez ordered that his remains be exhumed in order to determine "with the help of technological advances of the twenty-first and twentieth century" whether they are indeed Bolívar's or whether "the oligarchy stole Bolívar's bones."[20] ("The oligarchy" is one of those umbrella terms that Chávez uses for those he does not like: members of the opposition, foreigners, Americans, etc., whether or not they have any power or are actually rich.) The presidential commission charged with investigating the condition and whereabouts of Bolívar's bones is to be directed by Venezuela's vice president (incidentally, the sixth vice president that Chávez has appointed),[21] and to be composed of nine ministers from Chávez's cabinet and his attorney general, along with forensic experts.[22] Chávez is optimistic about his leads regarding the location of Bolívar's skull.[23] The blame for whatever may have happened, or not happened, to Bolívar and his bones is laid squarely on the United States, of course.[24]

At barely twenty years of age, Bolívar, like typical rich young Venezuelan men of his time, had embarked on a trip to Europe, where he spent over three years and became acquainted with the intoxicating ideas of some European fathers of liberalism. Bolívar's political decisions later in life, when he ruled over Venezuela and its neighboring territories, cast considerable doubt on his understanding of these doctrines. Chávez, in turn, has displayed a more glaring misunderstanding.

For example, Bolívar expressed particular admiration for Jeremy Bentham (1748–1832), the father of modern utilitarianism, whose "doctrine of utility became Bolívar's working philosophy," as John Lynch points out.[25] Utilitarianism, in brief, asserts that actions are good in proportion to their tendency to produce happiness for the greatest number of people. While many powerful objections have been raised against it, utilitarianism is an impressively resilient moral doctrine, as ever newer and subtler versions of it continue to be advanced. And yet Bentham's ideas came under attack during his own lifetime, even by the other modern champion of utilitarianism, John Stuart Mill (1806–1873).[26] Hardly anyone is a true Benthamite any longer. But Bolívar was Benthamite through and through, and while it could perhaps be argued that to criticize Bolívar for this would be somewhat anachronistic, what is undoubtedly anachronistic is to parrot Bolívar on the Benthamite lines today, as Chávez incessantly does.

One of Chávez's mantras is that "the most perfect government [meaning his own] is that which grants its citizens the greatest amount of happiness."[27] Chávez usually attributes this line to Bolívar—and to my knowledge has never acknowledged Bentham as the inspiration for it—but he alters and truncates Bolívar's words in significant ways. In his famous *Discurso de Angostura*, Bolívar said: "The most perfect system of government is that which produces the greatest amount of happiness, the greatest amount of social security, and the greatest amount of political stability."[28]

Chávez's replacement of Bolívar's verb meaning "to produce" with his own verb meaning "to grant" points to a much more paternalistic view of government. Happiness for Bolívar was not a gift that government graciously bestowed, but it is just that for Chávez. Then there is what Chávez leaves out. Rather obviously, Bolívar wanted to combine three elements that he found to be desirable: (1) happiness, (2) social security, and (3) political stability. Chávez simply omits two of these. I am not convinced that this move is intentional; it may simply be the result of ignorance. In any case, as I will suggest in the next chapter, Chávez's regime fails on all three counts in Bolívar's formula.

Consider another distortion, whereby Chávez turns Bolívar into a leader of the indigenous peoples, the slaves, and the downtrodden in general. Here are some telling passages in which Bolívar expresses his views on the native inhabitants of Latin America:

> The Indian is of such a relaxed temperament that he wishes only for repose and solitude; he does not even aspire to lead his tribe, much less to dominate other tribes. Happily, this species of man is the one that least demands a protagonist role [in political affairs], even though in numbers it surpasses the rest of all the other inhabitants [of Latin America]. This segment of the [Latin] American population is a sort of barrier containing the other parties; it does not seek authority, because it neither aspires to it, nor does it think of itself as capable of exercising it; this segment is content with peace, land, and family.[29]

The Indians, Bolívar says, "have never been able to avoid seeing the white man with anything other than great veneration, other than as beings favored by heaven."[30] Bolívar's views regarding slaves are similarly bleak:

[T]he slave in Spanish America vegetates abandoned in plantations, benefiting, if you will, from his own inaction, from his master's plantation, and from a considerable amount of the goods of liberty; and insofar as religion has taught him that to serve is a sacred duty, he has been born and has always existed in this domestic dependence, he considers himself in his natural state as a member of his master's family—whom he loves and respects.[31]

Bolívar made statements of this tenor in order to argue that it would be easy to attain peace in Latin America, given that these groups were conveniently peaceful and submissive. His description of the natives contradicts the portrayal of the fierce and brave Guaicaipuro (as an emblem for all Venezuelans) that has become part of a Venezuelan mythology, which Chávez systematically exploits. My goal is not to decide who is right about the indigenous or slave populations, but simply to point out the flaws and inconsistencies in Chávez's rendering of Bolívar.

Bolívar's attitude toward the Indians and the slaves was, to use John Lynch's characterization, "pragmatic, to say the least." Lynch quotes some rather eloquent passages from Bolívar's correspondence with another general of the period, Francisco de Paula Santander: "The more savage the Indians are the less they are missed for agriculture, industry, and so for society; yet their savagery does not prevent them from being good soldiers."[32] A few years later, Bolívar again confided in Santander:

I am convinced to the very marrow of my bones that [Latin] America can only be ruled by an able despotism.... We are the vile offspring of the predatory Spaniards who came to America to bleed her white and to breed with their victims. Later the illegitimate offspring of these unions joined with offspring of slaves transported from Africa. With such racial mixture and such a moral record, can we afford to place laws above leaders and principles above men?[33]

Whatever else one can say about these remarks, it is clear that they are not the words of a Marxist, nor of a champion of indigenous or downtrodden groups, nor even of a liberal. Yet Chávez is convinced that his alter-ego was all these things, and he has fooled many of the so-called experts on Venezuelan affairs, who now earn their livings writing hagiographic pamphlets on Chávez's behalf.

Consider what Gregory Wilpert, one of Chávez's panegyrists, tells us about Bolívar's relationship to Indians and slaves. Without the slightest shred of evidence, Wilpert flatly asserts that "compared to the theorists of the US American revolution, Bolívar was far more radical because of his opposition to slavery and his support for indigenous rights."[34] Wilpert's only source for such a bold and false claim is that Chávez *says* that Bolívar cared for slaves and indigenous peoples—excellent, trustworthy scholarship. The cover of Wilpert's book, *Changing Venezuela by Taking Power*, is adorned by a blurb from another Chávez fan, Noam Chomsky, who refers to the book as "outstanding, and highly informative."

Or consider Bart Jones's take on the Bolivian Constitution, which Bolívar drafted for Bolivia, the country that he named after himself: Jones approvingly tells us that "Bolívar drew up a constitution hailed as the most liberal in the world."[35] But Jones says not a word about who "hailed" it as such, or about the many critics in Bolívar's time and later who faulted this constitution for its tyrannical concentration of power. In fact, this constitution provided for a highly centralized executive branch in the hands of a lifelong appointee who would have the absolute right to choose his own successor. These were hardly liberal principles, of course, but none of this matters to Jones. Chávez *says* that Bolívar was a liberal hero, and that is all Jones needs.

Then there is Lisa Macdonald's claim—at an event organized by the Australia-Venezuela Solidarity Network and the Venezuelan embassy in Australia—that "Venezuela declared its independence following a long struggle led by the country's Indigenous people and a black slave revolt."[36] This is a blatant lie, nothing more.

It is unlikely that Chávez's misrepresentation of Bolívar is entirely due to ignorance, for he has tapped into the mythology about Bolívar to lend credibility to his own political agenda. The preexisting Bolívar cult is partly responsible for the ease with which Chávez's distortions are accepted. It also has served to keep a lid on most of what is critical of Bolívar in Venezuela, including two books written by Bolívar's contemporaries and published during his lifetime. One is by Gustavus Hippisley, who had been a colonel of the 1st Venezuelan Hussars, in addition to being a colonel-commandant of the British Legion in South America. The other book is by Henry La Fayette Villaume Ducoudray Holstein, who had been Bolívar's interim chief of staff. The two books were written, then, by people who knew Bolívar well.[37] Yet they are virtually unknown in Venezuela. Both were written in English, and to my knowledge there is no translation into Spanish of either one.

It takes no great perspicacity to see that this neglect may have something to do with the authors' negative portrayals of Bolívar. This is how Hippisley describes him:

> Bolívar's personal appearance is neither striking nor prepossessing. There is nothing about him, or belonging to him, either in manners, figure or conduct, to command attention.... Those who planted him in the situation he now holds were by turns his slaves and his victims, even under the mask of liberty, freedom, and independence. The smallness of his stature, and the meanness of his figure and physiognomy, would rather create contempt than respect. ... He possesses neither gratitude, honour, liberality, sympathy, nor humanity. ... He has neither talent nor abilities for a general, and especially for a commander in chief.... Tactic, movements, and manœuvre, are as unknown to him as to the lowest of his troops.... The victory which he gains to-day, however dearly purchased ... it is lost to-morrow, by some failure or palpable neglect on his part.[38]

Ducoudray Holstein's opinion of Bolívar is similar:

> [Bolívar] cannot walk long, but soon becomes fatigued. Wherever he goes his stay is short, seldom more than half an hour, and as soon as he returns, his hammock is fixed, he sits or lies, and swings upon it after the manner of his countrymen.... [There is nothing in Bolívar] which can inspire respect. When he wishes to persuade, or to bring anyone to his purpose, he employs the most seducing promises, taking a man by the arm, and walking and speaking with him, as with his most intimate friend. As soon as his purpose is attained,

he becomes cool, haughty, and often sarcastic; but he never ridicules a man of high character, or a brave man, except in his absence.... General Bolívar occupies himself very little in studying the military art. He understands no theory, and seldom asks a question, or holds any conversation relative to it.[39]

Maybe these books are not to be taken too seriously. John Lynch, whose expertise on Bolívar is unparalleled, chalks up Ducoudray Holstein as "malicious," a "foreign adventurer who did not get the promotion which he thought was his due."[40] Regarding Hippisley, Lynch tacitly suggests that he simply was not prepared for the difficulties of South American wars.[41] Maybe so, but for these books to be virtually unknown among Venezuelans, not even translated into Spanish, seems telling.[42] After all, the books are about Bolívar; at the very least, they contain interesting sociological and cultural remarks about Venezuela during his lifetime. Moreover, alongside the hagiographic literature on Bolívar that is normally read in Venezuela, these accounts, flawed as they may be, could nonetheless prove sobering.

My goal here is not to elucidate the "correct" assessment of Bolívar, but to show how Bolívar has been mythologized in ways detrimental to Venezuela and helpful to Chávez. This mythologizing has never been so extreme or so incoherent as in Chávez's hands. Indeed, Lynch ends his monumental biography of Bolívar with a discussion of how the authoritarian populist Chávez has exploited the cult of the Liberator:

The traditional cult of Bolívar had been used as a convenient ideology by military dictators, culminating in the regimes of Juan Vicente Gómez [1908–1935] and Eleazar López Contreras [1935–1941]; these had at least more or less respected the basic thoughts of the Liberator, even when they misrepresented their meaning. But the new heresy, far from maintaining continuity with the constitutional ideas of Bolívar, as was claimed, invented a new attribute, the populist Bolívar.... By exploiting the authoritarian tendency, which certainly existed in the thought and action of Bolívar, regimes in Cuba and Venezuela claim the Liberator as a patron for their policies, distorting his ideas in the process. Thus the Bolívar of liberty and equality is appropriated by a Marxist regime, which does not hold liberty and equality in high esteem

but needs a substitute for the failed Soviet model. And in Venezuela a populist regime of the twenty-first century, looking for political legitimacy, is
drawn to Bolívar as to a magnet, another victim of the spell. Who is to say
that it will be the last.[43]

Bolívar and Venezuelan Independence

Chávez's attempt to turn Bolívar into a Marxist-before-Marx visionary
is unsound, not only because there is virtually nothing in Bolívar's
thought or action that would justify such an effort, but also because
Karl Marx himself had a rather poor opinion of Bolívar. In a famous letter that Marx wrote to Frederick Engels, he referred to Bolívar as "the
most dastardly, most miserable and meanest of blackguards," and he
added "Bolívar is a veritable Soulouque."[44] Even for the notoriously
acrimonious Marx, these are hard words.[45]

Faustin-Élie Soulouque (1782–1867) was the ruler of Haiti from
1847 until he was deposed in 1859; from 1849 onward he was officially "Emperor Faustin I." An egocentric, nationalistic ruler, he tried to
concentrate all power in himself and his friends, for whom he created a
hereditary nobility. These traits and actions are common among strong
leaders, like Bolívar, and they are conspicuously present in Chávez.

Bolívar was involved in many if not most of Venezuela's painful and
protracted wars of independence. For Venezuela, independence cannot
accurately be dated; rather, historians tend to speak of an "independence
period" or "revolutionary period," from 1810 to 1830. Even though
Venezuelans had attempted to break from Spain since the late 1700s, it
was not until April 19, 1810, that the Province of Caracas, taking advantage of the political turmoil in Spain, declared itself independent.

Three things are important to highlight about this event. First, the
independence movement had almost nothing in the way of popular
support; historians agree that the population in Venezuela at this time
was indifferent on the subject. Second, this seizing of power was a
coup d'état—a bloodless one, but a coup nonetheless.[46] It was fitting

that Venezuela should become a nation in this way, for it was the first of many, many coups in the country's history. Third, technically speaking, this was not a legal declaration of independence; for that we must wait until July 5, 1811.

This first attempt at independence was short-lived. On July 25, 1812, scarcely two years after the coup of 1810, Venezuelan revolutionaries represented by Francisco de Miranda surrendered to the Royalists in San Mateo. The period between April 19, 1810, and July 25, 1812, is known among Venezuelan historians as the First Republic.

The revolutionaries did not give up, and Bolívar was at the forefront of the attempt to regain independence. On December 15, 1812, he wrote one of his most famous texts, the *Manifiesto de Cartagena*, which was the first important exposition of his views.[47] Here he discussed the reasons for the collapse of the First Republic, or, as it has sometimes been called, the *patria boba* ("foolish fatherland"), and he began to delineate the political views associated with him for the rest of his life. Above all, he blamed the failure of the First Republic on federalism and on what he saw as the limitations of the central government:

> [T]hat which most weakened the Venezuelan Government was the federal form it adopted, following the exaggerated maxims concerning the rights of man, which authorized him to rule himself, thus breaking the social contracts and rendering nations into anarchies.... The federal system, which may perhaps be the most perfect and the most capable of giving happiness to society, is, however, the most counter-indicated to the interest of our nascent states. Generally speaking, our fellow citizens are not yet ready to exercise their rights on their own.[48]

It is common, mainly among Venezuelan historians, to suggest that Bolívar later modified somewhat his jaundiced, mistrustful views about individuals and individual liberties. While there is perhaps some truth to this suggestion, Bolívar always remained a fervent proponent of strong, centralized rule—particularly if he was the ruler.

For example, late in his life Bolívar advocated the creation of a new country, which entailed breaking off what historically was a province of

Peru, known as Alto Peru (although at the time it was considered part of Rio de La Plata, and so still part of Spain). Bolívar himself was the first ruler of this new country, named Bolivia. The constitution that he drafted for Bolivia in 1826 was extraordinarily authoritarian.

In his famous *Discurso de Angostura,* Bolívar continued to voice his skepticism about individual liberty. Following an idiosyncratic reading of Rousseau, he argued that freedom "is a succulent meal, but of difficult digestion," and he added: "our feeble fellow citizens would have to strengthen their spirits long before they may be capable of digesting the healthy nutrients of liberty."[49] In fact, Bolívar was puzzled by the fact that the combination of federalism and respect for individual rights that he saw in the United States subsisted "so prosperously" and did not "collapse at the first sight of danger."[50]

In any case, Bolívar commanded another attempt to fight off the Spaniards. On June 15, 1813, he enacted the infamous *Decreto de Guerra a Muerte,* in which he promised to kill any Spaniard who did not actively cooperate with the revolution. (Venezuelans tend to argue that the Spaniards had long been killing civilians; but whether true or not, this is no justification for the immoral decree.) In spite of so radical a measure, Bolívar failed. Even so, it was during this brief period that he was given the title of "Liberator."

The Second Republic, which can be said to have begun roughly with the *Decreto de Guerra a Muerte,* came to an end quickly, just as the First Republic had. By December of 1814, after a series of major victories by the Royalists, the Second Republic fell. The independence movement was still not terribly popular, but rather a project that belonged above all to the rich white elite, a group that included Bolívar. One of the most feared Royalist commanders, José Tomás Boves (1782–1814), was in effect a hero of the dark-skinned natives, who fought fearlessly for him. Boves defeated some of the most important leaders of the independence movement, including Bolívar, before being killed on the field in the battle of Urica—which his forces nevertheless won.

Defeated, Bolívar and other leaders of the revolution once again retreated, though they would persevere still. By way of Nueva Granada (present-day Colombia), Bolívar fled to Jamaica and thence to Haiti. There he received considerable support from the president, Alexandre Pétion, who supplied all sorts of material aid to the efforts against the Royalists in Venezuela, from weapons and ships to money and a printing press. In exchange, Pétion asked Bolívar to abolish slavery in whatever territory he liberated. Bolívar complied as soon as he arrived in mainland Venezuela, on June 2, 1816. The period from around this date until December 17, 1819, is known as Venezuela's Third Republic.

Like its predecessors, the Third Republic was ephemeral. Its life was cut short not by military defeat at the hands of the Royalists, however, but by Bolívar's incorporating it into Colombia (and hence Panama) and Ecuador, forming a single nation called the "República de Colombia," which has gone down in history as "Gran Colombia." This entity lasted longer than Venezuela's three republics combined, almost ten years. But this did not mean that its existence was any less troubled; many problems afflicted Gran Colombia, not least of which was the desire of Venezuelans to secede from it. Things escalated to such a point that on August 27, 1828, Bolívar declared himself dictator and invested in himself the "supreme power" over Gran Colombia.[51] It is not difficult to see Bolívar's egotism at work: the solution to the problems of Gran Colombia was a strong leader, Bolívar himself, who should have immense power over his "immature" fellow citizens.

This is precisely the attitude that Chávez displays today. Some of Bolívar's most illiberal ideas, such as concentrating power in a centralized authority and opposing anything that remotely smacks of federalism, are the ones that Chávez most faithfully copies, besides parroting Bolívar's histrionics. Whether or not he was jealous of Bolívar, Ducoudray Holstein raised a criticism of him that sounds rather sensible: he pointed out that Bolívar's speeches were filled with the rhetoric of "profound submission to the will of the people, and above all, of a desire to resign his office." He notes that from 1814 to July 1828,

Bolívar "offered his resignation on every occasion" when he spoke in public, and yet "General Bolívar has never ceased to possess the supreme power." Ducoudray Holstein makes the obvious point that "a man who firmly resolves to resign power, is always able to do it."[52] There is a clear parallel with Chávez, who constantly offers to resign and subject himself to the will of the people, yet he remains in power.

Bolívar's dictatorship enjoyed some popular support, but not for long. In November of 1829, Venezuelan leaders announced their intention to break away from Gran Colombia. The following January, Bolívar stepped down as dictator, this time for real. A few months later, on December 17, 1830, he died of tuberculosis in Santa Marta, Colombia; he had planned to exile himself in Europe and had already sent some of his belongings ahead of him.

Here is an important difference between Bolívar and Chávez, who has *never* stepped down. Chávez's supporters around the globe boast of the many times he has bravely put his power on the line, subjecting himself to referenda and elections—a topic I will discuss in detail later. For now, I would just like to underscore the fact that Chávez was originally elected to be the president of Venezuela from March 12, 1999, until March 12, 2004; he has already more than doubled his term and keeps looking for ways to hold on to power indefinitely. Never has he been close to handing over power, and he boasts about remaining in office until the year 2021 and beyond.

Moreover, in spite of Bolívar's peculiar understanding of liberalism and his stubborn faith in strong, centralized government, he at least had the good sense to oppose long terms for the presidency. In fact, as he resigned from power in 1830, Bolívar claimed to regret having been forced to declare himself dictator in the first place. Much more famously, he unequivocally stated that "nothing is more dangerous than allowing one same person to remain in power for a long time: for the people get used to obey[ing] him, and he gets used to rul[ing] over them."[53] In this regard, Chávez is completely opposed to Bolívar.

There is one more difference between Bolívar and Chávez worth underscoring. As unsavory as Bolívar's paternalistic, strong-man political views may have been, and as nefarious as they proved to be during Venezuela's history, one can at least see a partial excuse, if not a justification, in light of Bolívar's situation. After all, he was trying to create a new nation, to liberate people from the colonial yoke, and in so doing he found himself fighting not only the inexperience of the people but also mighty Spain, one of the world's great military powers at that time. Chávez's strong-man mentality, in contrast, is utterly unjustified and obviously anachronistic.

The Revolution Has Been Televised— Time and Time Again

While the period of the Venezuelan independence movement was turbulent, it pales in comparison with Venezuelan history after 1830. I will briefly summarize this history up to the 1950s, and then discuss in more detail the period of stability and democracy that Venezuela enjoyed between the overthrow of the dictatorship of Marcos Pérez Jiménez in 1958 and Chávez's seizing of power in 1998.

Much of the pro-Chávez literature of late hails his Bolivarian Revolution as a substantial break with the past, inspired by the greatest Bolivarian ideals. I have already discussed some of the ways in which Chávez misappropriates Bolívar and ignores his central teachings. At the same time, Chávez's so-called "revolutionary" movement is no such thing. It is, rather, a grotesque throwback to the darkest hours of Venezuelan history.

As a matter of fact, "revolution" is a common word in Venezuelan history. The authoritative *Diccionario de Historia de Venezuela* has eighteen entries for the term; it discusses eighteen revolutions in Venezuelan history, excluding Chávez's alleged revolution. In addition, it lists ten rebellions, ten insurrections, five conspiracies, three revolts, and one uprising. Pedro León Zapata, Venezuela's most important cartoonist, had it exactly right when he published a cartoon in which Andrés Bello, as if drafting a dictionary, says, "When it refers to Venezuela, the word 'revolution' should be between scare quotes."[54] Consider the following lists of revolutions, rebellions, and insurrections, in chronological order:

Revolutions

The Revolution of April 19 (1810)

The Independence Revolution (1808–1823)

The Revolution of the Reforms (1835–1836)

The Popular Revolution (1846–1847)

The Liberal-Conservative Revolutions (1853–1854)

The March Revolution (1858)

The Federal Revolution (or Federal War) (1859–1863)

The Genuine Revolution (1867)

The Blue Revolution (1867–1868)

The Re-Conquering Revolution (another name for the Blue Revolution)

The April Revolution (1870)

The Revolution of Coro (1874–1875)

The Legalist Revolution (1892)

The Revolution of Queipa (1898)

The Liberal Restorative Revolution (1899)

The Liberating Revolution (1901–1903)

The Revolution of October 18 (1945)

Rebellions

The Rebellion of Negro Miguel (1553)

The Rebellion of Andresote (1731)

The Rebellion of San Felipe (1740–1741)

The Rebellion of the Commoners (1781)

The Rebellion of El Tocuyo (1744)

The Rebellion of Juan Francisco León (also listed under "Insurrections") (1749–1751)

The Rebellion of the Linares (1810)

The Royalist Rebellion (1813–1814)

The Rebellion of the Monagas (1831)

Insurrections

The Insurrection of Juan Francisco León (1749–1751)

The Insurrection of the Blacks in Coro (1795)

The Insurrection of Valencia (1811)

The Insurrection of the Islanders (1811)

The Insurrection of Barlovento (1812)

The Insurrection of Páez (1848–1849)

The Insurrection of April 7 (1928)

The Insurrection of Puerto Cabello (1962)

The Insurrection of Barcelona (also known as Barcelonazo) (1961)

The Insurrection of Carúpano (1962)

There have been many more acts of violence in Venezuelan history; this is just a collection of those that an authoritative source considers most important. It seems that the term "rebellion" is used more commonly for events before independence, whereas "revolution" is preferred for later events. Furthermore, three of the ten insurrections occurred between 1961 and 1962—not an insignificant fact, as we shall see. Needless to say, from a theoretical point of view it is hard to distinguish a rebellion from a revolution, or from an insurrection. While this sort of conceptual analysis may be important in a treatise on political theory, it is irrelevant to my purpose here, which is to convey the frequency with which Venezuelans have resorted to violence in order to advance whatever agendas they have in mind.

It should not be surprising, then, that Venezuela has had twenty-six constitutions since becoming independent. That Chávez refers to his movement as a "revolution" and has enacted a new constitution are, within the Venezuelan context, trite and tired gambits. Every Venezuelan dictator worth his salt has enacted at least one new constitution. When Chávez put forward his "Bolivarian Constitution" in 1999, he touted it as one of the most advanced in the world. Echoing Hitler's millennialism, he predicted that it would last a thousand years. Nine hundred ninety-two years too soon, however, he decided to amend his Bolivarian Constitution dramatically, via the referendum of December

2007. This attempt failed; but a year later, Chávez formally announced a new effort to amend the constitution—so as to allow himself a chance to stay in power indefinitely. This time he would succeed, as we shall see.

Even though the talk of revolution and the passing of a new constitution are perfectly common moves in Venezuela, Chávez's approach has some peculiarities. For one thing, the constitution that Chávez eliminated not only respected individual rights more clearly than any other in Venezuelan history, but also lasted the longest (1961–1999). Under the 1961 Constitution of the Republic of Venezuela, the country had the only significant period of political stability in its entire history. And this stability was precisely what Chávez brought to an abrupt end.

The first time a Venezuelan president elected by universal secret suffrage handed over power peacefully after his term ended was in 1964. This was Rómulo Betancourt, the most important figure of Venezuelan democracy, and indeed one of the most important political figures in Venezuela's history. Before Betancourt, on those rare occasions when the president had been elected, it was not by the people in general, but by a subset thereof: the Senate, or male voters, or landowners, and so on.

Many Venezuelan presidents were never elected: they simply took power by force. The majority of Venezuelan presidencies ended with a coup d'état, or in some way different from what had been stipulated when the presidency began. This happened in the following years: 1811, 1812 (twice), 1814, 1815 (twice), 1817, 1819 (three times), 1822, 1823, 1826, 1830 (twice), 1835 (twice), 1836, 1858, 1859 (twice), 1861, 1864, 1865, 1868 (three times), 1870 (twice), 1879, 1891, 1892, 1893, 1899, 1908, 1941, 1945, 1948, and 1958. With such a turbulent history, it is hard to be precise about these dates. But this list contains only the *successful* coups; a list including aborted or abandoned coups would be longer.

Against this backdrop, it is hard to overstate the accomplishments of the democratic era that followed the overthrow of the dictatorship of Marcos Pérez Jiménez on January 23, 1958. From that point onward, until Chávez led a failed coup in 1992, Venezuela enjoyed its most stable and prosperous period by far. In fact, it was the most secure and robust democracy in Latin America—which is astonishing for a nation with such a history of violence. Scholars use the term "exceptionalism" when discussing Venezuela during this period, and it truly was exceptional in the context of Latin American politics.

Readers may be surprised to learn that a book titled *The Venezuelan Democratic Revolution* was published as early as 1964, and that rather than dealing with Chávez's regime, it is about Rómulo Betancourt's government.[55] The similarity between Robert J. Alexander's book and any of the numerous pro-Chávez books written in the last few years ends with the word "revolution." Unlike Chávez's panegyrists, many of whom are only dimly aware of Latin American history, let alone Venezuelan history, Alexander was a renowned expert on Latin American affairs, and his book represents "a decade and a half of research."[56] He admitted that he had not written the book entirely "without a point of view or personal sympathies,"[57] but also acknowledged the "hundreds of people" who assisted him on his research. Among those he interviewed we find not only Rómulo Betancourt, then the sitting president of Venezuela and leader of the AD (Democratic Action) party, but also the main leaders of the opposition parties: Rafael Caldera of COPEI (Social Christian Party), Jóvito Villalba of URD (Democratic Republican Union), Jesús Farías of the Communist Party, and Domingo Alberto Rangel of MIR (Movement of the Revolutionary Left).

The characteristics of a normal democracy, such as an elected president transferring power at his term's end, were an absolute novelty in Venezuela before Betancourt's government. He handed over power in 1964, as he was supposed to do, to Raul Leoni, who in 1969 handed it over to Rafael Caldera (the candidate of the opposition), who in 1974 handed it over to Carlos Andrés Pérez (the candidate of the opposition), who in 1979 handed it over to Luis Herrera Campins (the candidate of the opposition), who in 1984 handed it over to Jaime Lusinchi (the candidate of the opposition), who in 1989 handed it over to

Carlos Andrés Pérez. Between Betancourt's presidency, which started in 1959, and Pérez's presidency, there were six peaceful transfers of power, four of which involved transferring power to the opposition.

Betancourt, the "father of Venezuelan democracy," governed the country in particularly difficult times. He was attacked both from the right, by militarist elements that suspected him of communist sympathies, and from the left, by those who saw him as too "bourgeois" and too friendly to the United States. In fact, Betancourt was attacked by the two most violent and notorious dictators in the twentieth-century Caribbean. He survived assassination attempts orchestrated by Rafael Leonidas Trujillo (AKA "Chapitas"), the right-wing strongman of the Dominican Republic between 1930 and 1961. The most famous of these attempts, in which Betancourt suffered severe burns, took place in Caracas on June 24, 1960. Betancourt also repelled many attempts of ideologues and guerrilla leaders backed by Fidel Castro to infiltrate Venezuela and export the "Cuban Revolution." These attempts culminated in the infamous "Machurucuto Incident" in 1967, during the government of Raul Leoni, when the Venezuelan armed forces engaged and fought off a group of Cuban guerrillas attempting to invade Venezuela.

Betancourt not only managed to survive during these turbulent years, but he also did so while respecting the rights of Venezuelans to an unprecedented degree. At the same time, he tried to turn Venezuela into a normal member of the international community. For example, he duly brought up Trujillo's attempts on his life, and Cuba's aggressions, before the Organization of American States, which in turn condemned these acts.[58]

The most serious threat to Betancourt came from the left-wing guerrillas (some actively supported by Castro's regime). They did not share Betancourt's respect for institutions, and they sought to overthrow his government. Things got so complicated for Betancourt that toward the end of his presidency, after one of many coup attempts (known as "El Carupanazo"), he suspended the operations of the

Communist Party and another left-wing party, MIR. This bolstered his opponents' claims that he was too repressive. But such accusations are unwarranted, as these parties admitted to carrying out illegal attacks on a legitimate government.

The pacification of Venezuela—that is, the pact between the left-wing guerrillas and the government—did not finally conclude until the first government of Rafael Caldera, who in the late 1960s offered broad amnesty to the guerrillas. The members of the guerrilla movements opted for participating in the democratic process through regular, nonviolent means. As part of this process, Caldera legalized the two parties that had been banned since the end of Betancourt's government. Some former guerrilla leaders, in fact, have become important figures in Venezuelan politics. Of course, although they have abandoned violence, some of them continue to believe in some of the left-leaning ideals that had motivated it.

But many of these former guerrilla leaders—for instance, Americo Martín and Teodoro Petkoff—now oppose Chávez. They object to his despotism, his authoritarianism, and his anachronistic political views. Indeed, many on Venezuela's left oppose Chávez quite strongly. It is mostly the global left (known in Spanish as *la izquierda boba* or "the foolish left") that takes Chávez to be a great hero.[59]

In addition to his role in the pacification process, Caldera is a particularly important figure in Chávez's story, for at least three reasons. First, Caldera emblematizes some of the things that went wrong with the Venezuelan democratic experience that began in 1958. While the leaders of the main political parties scrupulously adhered to the rule of law, institutional order, and election results, they nonetheless sought every possible *legal* way to seize power. Thus, from 1958 onward—in fact, since 1947—Caldera ran for president every single time it was not illegal for him to do so, except once, in 1988. While there is nothing legally inappropriate about this, it did impede the development of new leaders within the traditional political parties. Carlos Andrés Pérez, a top leader of Rómulo Betancourt's AD, governed Venezuela between

1974 and 1979, then ran once more in 1988, the first opportunity for him to do so again legally, and won.

Chávez thus shares with Caldera and Pérez (and Bolívar) the sort of messianic personalism whereby one thinks of himself as the only one capable of ruling the country. But unlike Chávez (and Bolívar, during the Venezuelan independence movement), leaders of the Venezuelan democracy did not attempt to keep themselves in power in perpetuity. None of these leaders ever extended his presidential term, or sought to allow for immediate or indefinite reelection, or tried to concentrate more and more power in his own hands.

The second reason for Caldera's importance is a speech he gave before the Venezuelan Congress on February 4, 1992, hours after Chávez led a coup attempt against Carlos Andrés Pérez's legitimate government, in which he came rather close to justifying it. Even if Caldera may have been right on more than one issue, many thought that this was not the moment for such a speech; it should have been a moment to oppose a bloody coup in no uncertain terms. Indeed, Caldera's speech stood in sharp contrast with the other speeches given that day, since virtually all members of Congress firmly condemned the coup.

Many Venezuelans speculated that Caldera's speech was a populist move, signaling his plans to run for president yet again in the 1993 elections. They were right. Although he lost the internal battle for the nomination of his own party, COPEI, Caldera chose to form a new party (National Convergence), and with the support of a motley group of smallish parties—some of which were led by the very guerrilla leaders to whom he had granted amnesty twenty-five years earlier—he ran again. And with a mere 30 percent of the vote, he again won the presidency.

The third reason why Caldera is important to our story is that, probably inspired by the success of his amnesties in the 1960s, he released Chávez from prison shortly after taking power. Many in Venezuela think this release was an impulsive miscalculation, while others think it was a continuation of the opportunism apparent in his speech to

Congress following Chávez's coup. The release came, first of all, barely a few months after Caldera was inaugurated in 1994, and before Chávez's trial had even begun—strictly speaking, it was not yet a pardon. Had Caldera waited until Chávez's conviction, Chávez would have been ineligible to run for president. After all, the evidence was incontrovertible. Chávez had proudly admitted to being the leader of the coup, which is now commemorated by a national holiday in Venezuela on a par with Independence Day and Bolívar's birthday. Of course, there was no guarantee that Chávez would not have seized power anyway, but it would have been more difficult. It would also have been harder for Chávez to maintain the democratic façade that he has kept up for many years.

The Collapse of Political Parties and the Demonization of the Past

In addition to Caldera's "pardon," Chávez's seizing of power in Venezuela was facilitated by the fact that the traditional political parties had become badly discredited. By running against COPEI in 1993, Caldera all but destroyed the party that he himself had created. Carlos Andrés Pérez's impeachment and resignation earlier in 1993 also contributed significantly to AD's demise. Corruption grew at an alarming pace, as did the clientelistic model of democracy that AD and COPEI had established. Whether in power or in the opposition, the traditional parties proved incapable of controlling the increasingly acute problems of Venezuelan society, such as inflation and crime. Thus, their once loyal followings began to dwindle.

With traditional parties weakened and socioeconomic problems mounting, the stage was set for a change. It could have been anyone, but Chávez effectively seized the moment. Venezuelans should have been wary of another militaristic strongman, but they were utterly fed up with their traditional parties. Never had they experienced as much stability and prosperity as they did with AD and COPEI, but they exhibited short memories and poor judgment. They voted for Chávez, and now, a decade later, they are still stuck with him. Some of the very problems that caused Venezuelans to grow disillusioned with AD and COPEI, and that Chávez himself criticized in the governments that came before his own, have worsened during his regime. Corruption, nepotism, and criminality have never been so rampant.

Still, as he campaigned for the presidency, Chávez needed more than simply to tap into the widespread disillusionment. He needed somehow to legitimize his attempted coup of 1992, which he has done by demonizing the democratic period that preceded him. He likes to dwell on a particular incident that he paints as a flaw in the democracy, although it wasn't such a bad thing at all.

On October 31, 1958, just about a month before the elections of December 7, the three main parties—AD, URD, and COPEI, the parties with the best chances of victory—voluntarily signed the famous "Pacto de Punto Fijo," named after Caldera's house in Caracas, where the leaders of the three parties met. Venezuelan toponymy is somewhat bizarre: Often, streets have no names but corners do; houses and buildings are typically known not by numbers but by names. "Punto Fijo" is also the name of a city in the western state of Falcón, which has misled some commentators to think it was there that the pact was signed.

"Punto Fijo," in addition, translates as "fixed point." Chávez and his followers have exploited the meaning of the words by trying to suggest that the pact was overly rigid and oppressive. This is like suggesting that a pact signed in Vermont speaks to its signatories' predilection for green mountains. No matter—Chávez's strategy has been to demonize the Pact of Punto Fijo and *puntofijismo* at all costs. And he has succeeded in this, convincing many, both in Venezuela and abroad, that the pact was responsible for all manner of ills.

The main argument against the pact is that it was an attempt to "limit the country's political system to competition between two parties," as Nikolas Kozloff puts it. Kozloff says that this pact was named after "the location Punto Fijo where COPEI and AD" put forth their exclusionary plans—without mentioning that this "location" was merely the personal residence of one of the signatories.[60] He also fails to mention that URD, a third party that seemed to stand a good chance of winning the elections (and which indeed finished in second place), also signed the pact.

Other commentators suggest that additional actors besides AD, URD, and COPEI participated in the Pact of Punto Fijo, such as "military, church, unions, [and] business."[61] D. L. Raby, unlike Kozloff, at least recognizes that URD was present at the meeting, but he echoes the idea that the pact was an agreement "to share power and patronage and ensure 'stability.'"[62] Raby's scare quotes around the word "stability" neatly capture the superficial understanding of Venezuelan history that characterizes Chávez scholarship lately. The tragicomic history of Venezuelan instability I have just sketched should more than justify the desire for stability that Raby so blithely mocks.

Richard Gott goes as far as calling the pact a "cynical agreement," a way to "keep up the pretense that Venezuela was 'a democracy.'" Gott further claims that the pact ensured that one party, "Acción Democrática, had the predominant and hegemonic role" and that another party, COPEI, "was allowed on occasion to win elections." The pact, Gott concludes, "effectively ensured that other parties, of left or right, would be prevented from ever taking power."[63] If the pact really ensured that no party other than AD or COPEI could win, how is it that Caldera won with his new party in 1994, defeating both of them? And how did Chávez win in 1998—again, defeating both AD and COPEI? Gott's suggestion that COPEI would "on occasion be allowed to win"—by whom? why? how?—doesn't make much more sense.

Similarly, Julia Buxton flatly asserts that the pact represented a "conservative consensus,"[64] and that it "created incentives for clientelistic practices and corrupt behavior," which mainly benefited AD and COPEI.[65] This focus on AD and COPEI is Chávez's modus operandi, for he wishes to discredit the two-party system that he claims was ushered in by the pact. But Chávez and his followers brazenly ignore the fact that *three* parties signed the pact, and the one that finished second in those elections (URD) was not one of what they call the "classic" two parties. We are denied an explanation, too, of why URD lost so much force in subsequent elections, even though it was an original signatory to the pact.

There is, however, a criticism of the Punto Fijo pact that is not as baseless as the complaints noted above. The signatories did not invite the Communist Party, which at the time was the fourth-largest party in Venezuela. But this criticism is not terribly serious, for at least three reasons. First, the Communist Party had thrown its support behind Wolfgang Larrazabal, the presidential candidate of URD, and so was at least indirectly involved in the pact. Second, the party was not the only one "excluded" from the pact, which grouped together only the parties that all the polls suggested had the best chance of winning the elections, and these parties joined in the pact voluntarily. In fact, the results of the elections confirmed the poll data, and thus retroactively justified the selection of the signatories. These are the results of the elections of 1958:

1. AD   1,275,973 votes, or 50 percent of the vote
2. URD   690,357 votes, or 27 percent
3. COPEI   392,335 votes, or 15 percent
4. PCV   160,791 votes, or 6 percent
5. IR   19,424 votes, or under 1 percent
6. PSV   15,457 votes, or under 1 percent
7. MENI   14,908 votes, or under 1 percent[66]

While it may be argued that the signatories of the Pact of Punto Fijo should have been more magnanimous, that they should have invited every other party (though this may have proven complicated, at least in logistical terms), they did collectively get over 92 percent of the popular vote. Third, those parties not invited to the pact were still perfectly capable of participating in the elections. All political parties were legal in Venezuela at the time.

It seems that those who, like Chávez, seek to demonize the Pact of Punto Fijo either do so disingenuously to advance an agenda, or have simply not read the text of the pact. Far from being an exclusionary or otherwise malefic document, it is rather innocuous: The brief text mostly contains desiderata for a better, more stable Venezuela. Above all, in what is the most concrete clause of the pact, the signatories agree to respect electoral results whatever they turn out to be.[67] The main goals of the pact were perfectly sensible, but within the context of Venezuelan history they were extraordinarily important. The pact decisively helped Venezuelans achieve what they had been unable to do during their country's tragic history of coup after coup: attain prosperity, stability, and progress.

Chávez's efforts to demonize the pact should not obscure the fact that it was a laudable accomplishment. What helped bring down the civility and respect for institutions that the pact fostered was Chávez's violent coup of 1992. It was, however, but the first step in a systematic process of demolishing Venezuelan democratic institutions, a process that Chávez would undertake in earnest after becoming president.

CHAPTER TWO

HUGO CHÁVEZ, THE MAN AND HIS REIGN

Most biographies, or rather hagiographies, of Chávez begin by emphasizing the fact that he was extremely poor as a child and adolescent, that he grew up in a mud hut, far away from any big city, and so on. It's a trite trope with which we are all familiar: rags to riches.[1] The hardships of his childhood are highlighted for two main reasons. First, it is a way to set Chávez apart from the Venezuelan presidents of the much-maligned *ancien régime*. Second, it enhances the mythology of the climb from obscurity, the heroic triumph over adversity, that befits a larger-than-life Great Leader.

But in his socioeconomic background, Chávez does not differ significantly from his predecessors. In this respect, Bolívar was an anomaly among Venezuelan rulers. In particular, the elected leaders of the democratic period immediately preceding Chávez (Rómulo Betancourt, Raul Leoni, Rafael Caldera, Carlos Andrés Pérez, Luis Herrera Campins, and Jaime Lusinchi) were all from rather humble origins. Moreover, with the exception of Betancourt, who was born in Guatire, a sleepy satellite town on the outskirts of Caracas, all the other presidents were, like Chávez, born in Venezuela's provincial towns.

Chávez and his hagiographers like to emphasize that Chávez is also racially different from his predecessors. In his *Cowboy in Caracas,* Charles Hardy comments that "one of Chávez's problems as president is that he is proud of his *mestizo* [mixed] blood."[2] Predictably, Hardy accuses those who oppose Chávez of being "racists." But virtually all of Chávez's predecessors (again, with the notable exception of Bolívar) were *mestizos* as well, and they did not seem one bit less "proud" of their ethnic background than is Chávez. Given that Venezuela was, and continues to be, a country in which the overwhelming majority of the population is of "mixed race," the dynamics of race relations there are rather different from the dynamics in, say, the United States. Chávez is no darker than many of his predecessors, nor is he darker than many of those who oppose him. Claudio Fermín, for example, who had been elected the mayor of Caracas long before Chávez's 1992 coup, and who has always opposed Chávez, is much darker than Chávez. Fermín has always been fondly known as "El Negro Fermín." In Venezuela, to call someone *negro* or *negra* is often a sign of affection.

The central assertions of the usual hagiographies of Chávez are false. Chávez does not differ significantly from his predecessors in terms of his place of birth, his socioeconomic background, or his ethnicity. These similarities between Chávez and his predecessors cast doubts on the other goal of the hagiographies: There is nothing particularly heroic or even unusual about his ascent to power. Chávez did rise from a humble background, but in this he was no different from most Venezuelan presidents, politicians, and military men.

Social mobility was among the successes of the Venezuelan democracy into which Chávez had been born. Not only had many Venezuelans (and immigrants) succeeded in climbing the socioeconomic ladder, but they had also done so, like Chávez, by making use of state-subsidized educational institutions. Chávez incessantly criticizes the democratic system he sought to end by force in 1992, but he never mentions that this system allowed him to attend public schools like the Liceo O'Leary in Barinas, and then Venezuela's Military Academy.

Not all educational programs in Venezuela were particularly impressive. While the efforts of the pre-Chávez democratic governments in the field of education bore fruit in the sense of making education more accessible, these efforts were not unqualified successes. In addition to inefficiency, bureaucratization, and corruption, all of which were prevalent during the democratic period, Venezuelan education faced the problem of losing quality with expanding accessibility. As more and more instructors were needed to educate more and more students, the standards fell lower and lower. Public high schools, which in the 1950s and 1960s had been the obvious choice for middle-class Venezuelans, became an unthinkable option from the 1970s onward, and universities fared no better.

Consider Chávez's own remarks about the Venezuelan Military Academy, which was, at least since 1958, supposed to be a university-level institution. According to Chávez, however, in the 1960s students were accepted into the Military Academy while they were still in middle school, and graduation from the Academy (with the rank of second lieutenant) would follow admission "immediately," or in just "two years."[3] Chávez speculates that the feeble admission "procedures" and the ridiculously expedited coursework resulted from the struggles of the Venezuelan government's efforts to fight the guerrilla movements; one can only imagine those "fifteen-year-old second lieutenants"[4] fighting the guerrillas. But the rather lax admission standards, as well as the debatable standards of the curricula, became increasingly problematic in most Venezuelan educational institutions, not just in the Military Academy.

In any case, Chávez almost proudly admits that he failed chemistry in high school; he chalks this up to the fact that he "did not like" chemistry.[5] His failure in this subject meant that in theory he was ineligible to enter the Military Academy, which had the rank of a university and required at least a high school diploma. Chávez had not finished high school, yet he was admitted. (The Military Academy's yearbook reports that Chávez had a tendency to sleep during class.)[6] This is Chávez's own recollection of the admission process:

At that point an Officer told us that the only chance we had to be provisionally accepted was to be good in sports.... A while later they began asking for those who played baseball, and the first applicants to be consulted were us, the kids who had flunked High School courses.... The first test was to get dressed like a ball player; they pointed to the dugout and the uniforms, and they began observing those who were able to get inside the uniforms faster. I had just returned from a [baseball] national tournament, so I had no difficulties with this. In such a way began the selection of those who would dress and leave [the dugout] the fastest, and those who did not know how to get the uniform on were eliminated.[7]

Chávez tells a protracted story about how he failed as a pitcher that day, since he was sore from having pitched a game just three days before. Luckily, he was given an opportunity to bat, and he hit three balls against the outfield wall (a very good thing in baseball). He concludes:

This is how I was admitted into the Military Academy; if I had not played well, I would not have been admitted.... This is how I entered the military world, which was at the time entirely unknown to me.... I did not understand much, but I was motivated by that hope of being there in order to eventually become a baseball player.[8]

Perhaps more amazing than the process of selection itself was the way in which the majority of Venezuelans reacted to it. Chávez's story is contained in a book that is very famous in Venezuela: *Habla el Comandante* ("The Commander Speaks"), assembled by the renowned Venezuelan historian and journalist Agustín Blanco Muñoz. I say "assembled" because the book, released before Chávez was elected in 1998, is essentially a long interview. A large number of Venezuelan readers seemed indifferent to Chávez's smart-alecky tale of gaining admission into an alleged university without a high school diploma. Like Chávez, they were oblivious to what it says about the integrity of Venezuela's elite school for military officers.

It is easy to speculate that this indifference is in no small part a *result* of the erosion of academic standards that afflicted Venezuela in the past fifty years. One need only skim through a judicial decision in Venezuela during that time to see the signs of incompetence and ignorance.[9] Many Venezuelan judges and Supreme Court justices seem unable to spell (and Spanish is, by and large, a phonetic language with rather simple spelling rules). Forming grammatical, coherent sentences seems even more difficult among members of the Venezuelan judiciary, as would be painfully obvious to anyone witnessing a session of Venezuela's National Assembly.

I will return to the peculiarities of Venezuela's educational system later on. For now I wish to continue sketching aspects of Chávez's personal life. There have been several women of note in Chávez's life. Perhaps the most important of them all is his grandmother Rosa Inés, whom he credits with teaching him Venezuelan history. By any account, the second most important woman in Chávez's life is Herma Marskman, who was his mistress for over ten years (roughly between 1984 and 1994) and an important member of the early conspiratorial groups that Chávez organized in the armed forces.[10] Marskman claims that Chávez wanted to divorce Nancy Colmenares, his first wife, and even to have a child with her (Marskman). She allegedly became pregnant with Chávez's baby, but had a miscarriage.[11] While Chávez has avoided talking much about his relationship with Marskman, he has refused to deny that the pregnancy occurred, even when asked about it point blank.[12] Marskman claims that she considered her relationship with Chávez to have ended when, during an interview in 1994, he presented himself as a "model family man" and credited his wife Nancy with supporting him, when in fact it was Marskman who had stood by his side all those years.[13] Marskman has accused Chávez of betraying their noble revolutionary dreams and becoming a typical narcissistic dictator.[14]

Marskman's accusation of narcissism is not the result of a scorned woman's bitterness. It is an apt description of Chávez, used by many other commentators, such as Reiner Luyken in "Der Narziss von Caracas," and Andrés Oppenheimer, who wittily refers to Chávez's project as "Narcissist-Leninist."[15] The accusation also explains the joke, common among Venezuelans, wherein their president is called "Ego Chávez"—"ego" and "Hugo" sounding more alike in Spanish than they do in English.

Nancy Colmenares has been an obscure figure. Very little is known about her, other than that she was married to Chávez for fifteen years and bore him three children. (Chávez was involved with Marskman for ten of those fifteen years.) His second wife, Marisabel Rodríguez, is much better known, and she served as First Lady for the first few years of Chávez's regime. Marisabel was the victim of one of Chávez's most famous remarks as president, a remark that speaks to the way in which Chávez treats women. On Valentine's Day, Chávez, on national television, told her to prepare herself: *"Esta noche te doy lo tuyo."*[16] Literally, the expression means "Tonight I will give you what is yours," but the colloquial sense, together with Chávez's body language, made its meaning on the occasion quite clear to every Venezuelan: "Marisabel, prepare for rough sex tonight."

During the years following her divorce from Chávez, Marisabel kept a low profile and avoided saying anything negative about him. Recently, however, she has broken her silence and has accused him of, among other things, neglecting their daughter. Chávez had sued her for expanded visitation rights, which include the obligation for Marisabel to hand over the young girl to emissaries from Chávez (rather than to Chávez himself). Shortly after this, however, Chávez desisted from the lawsuit, arguing that it would make his daughter suffer. He announced his decision to give up the lawsuit on national television during one of his interminable (often in excess of seven hours) *Aló Presidente* shows. Chávez accompanied this announcement with a histrionic and self-serving performance of the famous biblical passage where King Solomon offers to cut in half a baby claimed by two prostitutes, a proposal intended to prompt the true and false mothers to reveal themselves—for a real mother would sooner give up her child to another woman than let it be murdered. Chávez identified himself with the baby's true mother, who was willing to surrender her rights out of love for her child.[17]

Marisabel's version of events is rather different. She claims that after their divorce, Chávez has become a deadbeat father. She also says that while they were married, Chávez subjected her to psychological abuse and "would have liked" to inflict physical abuse on her as well. "Chávez did not beat me up," she says, "because I did not let him."[18]

Chávez's relationship with women is characterized by a special vulgarity. One of his favorite targets was Condoleezza Rice, whom he often called "Condolence" and more frequently "Little Girl." Not only did Chávez often claim that Rice was in love with him, but he compounded the insult by suggesting that while he would give his very life for Venezuela, it would be "too much of a sacrifice" to have sex with Condoleezza (which purportedly she would desperately want).[19] More recently Chávez lashed out against Germany's chancellor, Angela Merkel, whom he accused on national television of being a Nazi, and whom, again on national television, he told to go to hell—to the joyful paroxysms of his delirious audience.[20]

Chávez's misogynistic ways are part and parcel of his *über*-macho image. He proudly presents himself as the always-ready stallion, attacking his opponents by calling them *bate-quebrao*, an expression that literally means "broken-bat," the rough equivalent of "limp-dick." A song frequently overheard in Chávez's popular meetings is called "Palo por ese culo," which has become a sort of rallying cry of the Chavista movement and translates simply as "a stick up that ass."[21]

Most pro-Chávez commentators either entirely avoid discussing Chávez's misogyny, or they chalk it up as the charming flamboyance of the Great Macho. For example, Bart Jones tells us, if not approvingly then at least indifferently, about comrades joking that Chávez in his youth "couldn't see a broomstick in a skirt because he would fall in love."[22] Jones seems to celebrate the notion that there are "long lines of women anxious to throw themselves at El Comandante."[23] He also tells us that Chávez has had "a reputation as a ladies' man," to which he adds that such a reputation was "not unusual in Venezuela, where few marriages were exclusive arrangements."[24] Needless to say, this remark not only lacks a basis in evidence, but also insults the Venezuelans who do not cheat on their spouses.

Jones's indifference to Chavez's vulgarity and dishonesty is particularly noteworthy given the fact that he has been a member of the Maryknoll Catholic missionary movement, and one would have expected at least a modicum of decorum from a member of such a religious organization. (Maryknoll seems to have a powerful attraction to Chávez's revolution: another Maryknoll operative in Venezuela, Charles Hardy, also writes pamphlets in support of Chávez, and Maryknoll operatives are in frequent communication with Chávez's salaried lobbyists in Washington.)[25] Jones insults Chávez's first wife, Nancy, when he justifies Chávez's relationship with his best-known mistress, Herma Marskman, by telling us that "she was a serious woman, an intellectual"—unlike his wife, we are led to believe.[26] (Insults are cheap in the pro-Chávez camp.) Jones's assessment of Marskman's intellectual seriousness is not affected by Marskman's fondness for tarot cards and palm readers.[27]

Richard Gott admits that he, like other "reporters," is "susceptible to the charms of Latin America's strong men," and says that Chávez is "an attractive and audacious colonel," even more charismatic than his predecessors.[28] Moreover, Gott has the effrontery to insult Venezuelans in general, nonchalantly telling us that Venezuela is "a society of gangsters and looters."[29]

All in the Family

One particularly consequential aspect of Chavez's relationship with his family is nepotism—something that is not new to Venezuela, but which has never run as high as during Chávez's presidency. His family is widely known in Venezuela as "the royal family," in light of the immense power it now wields. To be sure, nepotism is rampant in

Venezuela beyond Chávez's immediate family; almost any Chavista worth his salt has to show that he can help relatives secure jobs in the revolutionary government.

A complete list of these nepotistic champions would take hundreds of pages; but a short list of the most prominent figures would include Diosdado Cabello (whose name in English is "God-given Hair"), perhaps Chávez's strongest ally. Cabello has held many offices in Chávez's government, including vice president of Venezuela and governor of Miranda, the country's most populous state. He has found jobs for his younger brother, José David, at the helm of important offices including the Venezuelan Tax Revenue Office and the Customs Office at Venezuela's main airport. José Vicente Rangel, former vice president, minister of defense, and foreign minister, managed to get his son, José Vicente Rangel Avalos, elected mayor of one of Caracas's most important boroughs. The current foreign minister, Nicolás Maduro, is married to Cilia Flores, the speaker of the National Assembly—a position he himself had held just before her. And on and on … but I promised a brief list.

The shamelessness of such nepotism was obvious from the very beginning of Chávez's regime. Back in 1999, allegations surfaced that José Vicente Rangel, who was then the chancellor and one of Chávez's main advisors, had been giving diplomatic posts to Chávez's cronies. Rangel confessed to the charge, but defended himself by claiming that it was only *asking* for favors that was reprehensible, not granting them.

The example of Rangel also highlights the dizzying pace with which Chávez transfers personnel from one office to another. The expression "cabinet shuffle" is a laughable understatement when it comes to Chávez. Hardly a month goes by without his changing some of his ministers, or creating new ministries by decree, or eliminating, merging, or splitting ministries on the spur of the moment. Hardly a week goes by when he doesn't subcontract out this or that public servant. He who was in charge of education yesterday is in charge of taxes today, and the next day he will be the ambassador to the Vatican. She who was in charge of labor relations yesterday is today in charge of a police department, and tomorrow of hospitals. One needn't be especially perceptive to suspect that very few people have the qualifications and skills in so many different areas as to be competent heads of so many disparate offices.

This shuffling of personnel reached a nadir of absurdity with the case of Jorge Rodríguez, the president of Chávez's United Socialist Party, the PSUV (Chávez had ordered all the parties that supported him to merge into a single party), and later mayor of one of the main boroughs of Caracas. Rodríguez had been the chairman of Venezuela's National Electoral Council, supposedly a nonpartisan organization whose job is to oversee the elections. According to pamphlets distributed by the Venezuela Information Office, one of Chávez's lobbying groups in Washington,

> Venezuelan elections are overseen by a National Electoral Council (known as the "CNE" for its Spanish acronym). Under the Venezuelan Constitution, the CNE is a branch of government separate from the Executive, Legislative or Judicial branches, and as such is better protected from political biases or pressure. Today, the CNE board is made up of technical experts.[30]

During the referendum to oust Chávez in 2004, however, the opposition alleged that there were many irregularities in the Electoral Council, all of which benefited Chávez's regime. Naturally, Chávez denied any wrongdoing. A few months after the referendum, Jorge Rodríguez left his post as chairman of the council; Chávez had appointed him vice president. Another "technical expert" who went straight from the CNE to a cushy job within Chávez's regime was Francisco Carrasquero, who was rewarded for his services as chairman of the council with a post as a justice on the Supreme Court (the Supreme Tribunal of Justice), a position that he may enjoy in perpetuity.

Chávez's immediate relatives have held various positions either in government or in banks and other institutions that benefit immensely from their interaction with the government. Chávez's second wife,

Marisabel, ran for the National Assembly before they divorced, and she won the second-highest vote total of any candidate in the country. Adán Chávez, Hugo's older brother, has been the secretary of education, the ambassador to Cuba, and the press secretary in the Office of the President, among many other positions. Another brother, Argenis, has been the deputy governor and secretary of state in the state of Barinas, a position newly invented just for him. The governor of the state for many years was, not surprisingly, also a Chávez: Hugo de los Reyes Chávez, the president's father, though he has now been substituted by Adán Chávez. Adelis Chávez, another brother, has been a banker with Sofitasa, a bank that thrives on governmental accounts; previously he had been appointed (by the Great Leader himself) chairman of the organizing committee for the Copa America, the most important soccer tournament in the Americas, which for the first time in history took place in Venezuela in 2007. (Venezuela has always been the weakest South American soccer selection.) Ignacio Chávez, another brother, also wears many hats: he has been in charge of one of the many Venezuelan-Cuban agreements on health, and has also been a council man in Barinitas, a city in the state of Barinas. The last and youngest of Chávez's brothers, Anibal Chávez, is the mayor of Sabaneta, Chávez's birthplace.

In a recent article in the *Washington Post,* it was asserted that the Chávez family had "made a personal fiefdom of this State."[31] If there was any inaccuracy in this pronouncement, it was in its understatement: Chávez and his family have turned not just Barinas but the entire country into their personal fiefdom.

Elena Frías de Chávez, the mother of the Great Leader, deserves special mention. Since Chávez was divorced from Marisabel, his mother has occupied the role traditionally given to Venezuelan First Ladies: directorship of the Children's Fund. What is most striking about Elena is the metamorphosis she has undergone in the sort of clothes that she wears and the ostentatious jewelry that she now sports. It is evident, too, that she has lost a lot of weight and has had plastic surgery. Now, I have nothing against jewelry, luxury cars, or plastic surgery, but it is difficult to ignore the inconsistency between Chávez's discourse against capitalism and consumerism, on the one hand, and the conspicuous consumption practiced by Chávez and his immediate relatives, on the other.

Similarly inconsistent with the revolution's supposedly lofty goals is that Chávez's most trusted aides have been involved in a host of corruption scandals, in spite of Chávez's spirited denunciation of the corruption cases in previous regimes. It is easy to see why Venezuelans refer to Chávez's *revolución* as a mere *robolución,* a word made up by combining the noun for "revolution" with the verb meaning "to steal." They also mock its "socialist" aspect as simply giving rise to a new "Boliburguesia," a word concocted by melding "Bolivarian" with "bourgeoisie," suggesting that Chávez's revolution has resulted in a new Bolivarian oligarchy.

The Virtues of the Ruler and the Fruits of Chávez's Regime

Chávez's personal dishonesty has encouraged blatant contempt for truth throughout his regime. That Chávez both knows how to lie and is accustomed to doing so can no longer be doubted: A perennial conspirator (as we shall see) and an adulterous husband, he has been lying all his adult life. The institutionalized dishonesty of his regime thus serves to advance whatever story will highlight the supposed successes of his revolution. Here are two examples from a virtually inexhaustible reservoir, the first relating to education and the second to crime control.

Chávez has claimed that through the "Misión Robinson," his government has been able to teach "over 1.5 million illiterate Venezuelans" to read and write, and that Venezuela has become a land "free of illiteracy." (Most of Chávez's plans are called "missions," as his limited, overly militaristic vocabulary has invaded every nook and cranny of an impoverished Venezuelan discourse. Thus there are "battalions" to bring food, "platoons" to teach home economics, "squadrons" to clean streets, "patrols" to count votes, and so forth.) Figures such as the 1.5 million taught to read are mainly the fruit of Chávez's wild imagination, though they are shamelessly repeated by his acolytes and apologists.[32] In general, it is hard to find reliable information from Venezuelan official sources, and not only because of the mendacity of Chávez's regime, but because these sources do not seem to be able to stick to one single story. In his capacity as secretary of education, Adán Chávez, one of Hugo's brothers, has admitted that the official literacy figures have been erroneous.[33]

A previous secretary of education, Aristóbulo Isturiz, had backpedalled on Chávez's grandiose claims and tried to tone down his declaration that the United Nations had certified that "Venezuela had become a territory free from illiteracy."[34] Skeptics doubted the assertion, and Isturiz retorted by saying that "Venezuela is a sovereign nation" and that it does not need the United Nations, or any other organization, to declare it to be this or that. "In an act of sovereignty," Isturiz asserted, "Venezuela declares itself to be free of illiteracy."[35] But he evaded the point that Chávez was wrong in saying that the United Nations had certified Venezuela to be free of illiteracy.

Isturiz had been present at a memorable pedagogical session that Chávez held with elementary school children. Chávez misspelled a common verb, *adquirir* (to acquire), as *adquerir*. Horrified, his minister of education made all sorts of gestures, coughing and wheezing, to get the Great Leader's attention. But Chávez didn't notice Isturiz's gesticulations soon enough, and he proceeded to declaim on the misspelled word's etymology and meaning. Since *adquerir* looks like *querer* (to want, to love), Chávez asserted, in front of an understandably stupefied audience, that "to acquire means something like wanting, but going beyond it."[36]

In another pedagogical moment, Chávez alluded to a famous passage from the Gospel of Matthew: "It is easier for a camel to go through the eye of a needle, than for a rich man to enter into the kingdom of God."[37] There were children in the large auditorium where he was pontificating, and he asked them, "Do you kids know what a camel is?" One child answered in the affirmative by saying, "Yes, it is an animal that lives in the desert." All arrogance, Chávez one-upped the five-year-old: "And in the jungle, too, kiddo." Camels, he added, can be "as big as the auditorium itself."[38] Was Chávez simply confusing camels with dinosaurs? It would not have been his biggest mistake.

Chávez's claims for the educational achievements of his Bolivarian Revolution may be evaluated against data from international organizations like the United Nations. The UN's *Human Development Report 1999*, which contains the latest figures for the period immediately preceding Chávez's rule, listed Venezuela's literacy rate at 92 percent and the country itself as number forty-eight worldwide in the Human Development Index. After about ten years of the Chávez regime, Venezuela's literacy rate is listed at 93 percent, and the country is number seventy-four worldwide in the Human Development Index.[39]

The Venezuelan population in 1999 was slightly over twenty-one million, and if we exclude the roughly one-third of the population below fifteen years of age (a segment that does not count for the UN's statistics on literacy), then the universe of Venezuelans who could have been taught to read and write was about fourteen million. And since the UN's increase in the Venezuelan literacy rate is a mere 1 percent, it follows that in ten years, Chávez's regime has taught, at best, around 140,000 people to read and write. This is a rather underwhelming number. During the same period, neighboring Colombia raised its literacy rate from 90.9 percent to 92.8 percent, an increase almost twice what Venezuela showed. Mired in a veritable civil war, Colombia nevertheless brought literacy to about 560,000 Colombians, while Chávez, with his much-touted Bolivarian Revolution and with stratospheric oil revenues, didn't even approach that number. Moreover, the figures that Chávez offers regarding the literacy rate are inflated more than tenfold: from around 140,000 to "at least 1,500,000," which is the official figure. This sort of gross exaggeration—not to call it a flat-out lie—is par for the course in Chávez's regime.

While he lies about literacy rates, Chávez has ordered a deceptive "revamping" of the Venezuelan educational system. Predictably, the new curriculum rewrites history, crowning Chávez as the savior of the country, a veritable new Bolívar. It also presents history in Chávez's favorite Manichean terms, with the United States as the most formidable source of evil in the world and the quintessential enemy of Venezuela, which by contrast is pure goodness. Answering critics who claim that his new system is but a means to indoctrinate Venezuelan youth, Chávez claims that he is proud of this indoctrination, that no education is possible without indoctrination. He is simply replacing the old "Eurocentric system that forced us to admire Tarzan, Clark Kent, Mandrake the Magician, and the Phantom"[40] with a new Bolivarian-socialist scheme.[41]

Chávez, as usual, has it wrong. All these characters were created by Americans, in the United States; there is nothing "Euro" about them. And I have never met a Venezuelan who had ever heard of a Venezuelan school curriculum in which students were supposed to study American cartoon characters, much less required to venerate them. The battle against Tarzan and Clark Kent is a classic case of politics by straw man. Some American cartoons do regularly appear on Venezuelan television; but Chávez found *The Simpsons* immoral and corrupting to Venezuelan children, so he ordered it off the air. It is hard to understand Chávez's priorities when it comes to educational values, since the show that replaced *The Simpsons* is none other than the enlightening, uplifting *Baywatch*. Perhaps a show about women with surgically modified breasts running around in bikinis reminds Chávez of one of his passions during his time in the military: beauty pageants.[42] In his mind, at least, there is more pedagogical value in *Baywatch* than in *The Simpsons*.

Chávez's main contribution to education in Venezuela has been to brainwash an entire generation of a country located relatively close to the United States into believing that it is a dictatorship, "the evilest empire that has ever existed on the face of the earth," and the quintessential enemy.[43] And yet, many Americans do not worry about Chávez, but enthusiastically praise him for his innumerable achievements in education.

Another area where Chávez claims great success for his revolution is in controlling crime, which has been a major and escalating problem in Venezuela at least since the 1960s. In fact, crime has gotten much worse during Chávez's regime.[44] But just as in the case of education, Chávez has attempted to change the reality by altering the statistics and muddying the waters with confusing categories. For example, when counting the number of homicide victims, the regime excludes those who were killed "resisting authority." This category encompasses a hodgepodge of casualties: killed by the police, killed in street fights, killed in strange circumstances, and so on. During a recent interview, Ramón Rodríguez Chacín, who was then Chávez's secretary of the interior and citizen's security, claimed that those killed as a result of gang violence should not be counted as victims of homicide. Moreover, he said, such killings do not really show any increased level of insecurity in the country, for only gang members are affected. Thus, you would feel insecure "only if you yourself are a gang member."

Venezuela's most important human rights organization, PROVEA (Program of Education-Action in Human Rights), has compiled data on murder since 1990—based, in turn, on official government statistics and on statistics from Venezuela's main national university.[45] The table on the next page shows that crime, already a problem before Chávez took office in February 1999, grew much worse after he seized power. (Figures for Chávez's years are in boldface.) During the first seven years that Chávez was in power, 100,000 people were killed in Venezuela, a country with scarcely more than twenty million inhabitants. The number of crime-related deaths in Venezuela since 2000, Chávez's first full year in power, has averaged about 15,000 per year (assuming, naïvely,

Year	Homicide	Resisting Authority	Unclear	Total
1990	2474	313	N/A	2787
1991	2502	322	3437	6261
1992	3266	399	3619	7284
1993	4292	485	3411	8188
1994	4733	732	N/A	5465
1995	4481	592	N/A	5073
1996	4961	657	3358	8976
1997	4225	671	3361	8257
1998	4550	609	3461	8620
1999	5968	607	3474	10049
2000	8022	943	3467	12432
2001	7960	1251	3801	13012
2002	9617	1720	3752	15089
2003	11342	2305	3891	17538
2004	9719	2150	4031	15900
2005	9964	1355	4158	15477

that all cases are reported), and there is no sign whatsoever that things are improving.[46] As a sobering comparison: by August 21, 2008, over five years after the war in Iraq commenced, the total number of American casualties was 4,148, and in Afghanistan the number was 574.[47]

An average of 15,000 murders a year means forty-four murders a day, almost two per hour. If one adds up all the deaths that Chávez's regime seeks to conceal, the rate of homicide victims per year is fifty-seven per 100,000 inhabitants.[48] This figure would mean that Venezuela's murder rate is the highest in the world—that it is the most dangerous place on the face of the earth.[49] Yet Chávez shamelessly says the suggestion that Venezuela is unsafe at all, or more unsafe than it was before he seized power, is "a lie the size of a cathedral."[50]

Here are two instances of demonstrable failure in Chávez's regime, but almost any indicator would show similarly abysmal results. For example, public hospitals in Venezuela seem to be worse than they were before Chávez, public transportation even more chaotic, and so on.[51] Economic freedom is virtually nonexistent in Venezuela. The Heritage Foundation's Index of Economic Freedom shows Venezuela falling year after year since Chávez took power. In its 2008 report, Venezuela occupies the 148th place out of 157 countries evaluated.[52] In the 1998 ranking, the last year before Chávez seized power, Venezuela was 97th out of 156 nations,[53] not stellar but much better than after a decade with Chávez.

Corruption was one of the greatest maladies of the democratic period in Venezuela—and one which Chávez exploited in his successful campaign to become president. But it has never been worse than it is under Chávez's regime. In 2007, Transparency International examined 179 nations around the globe, measuring degrees of corruption: Venezuela came out at number 162 (with the highest number being the most corrupt).[54] In the table for 1999, the first year of Chávez's regime, Venezuela had been number 75 out of 99 nations,[55] not great but better than after a decade with Chávez.

Chávez ran for president on an explicit promise to reduce the number of ministries. In 1988, when there were sixteen ministries in the Venezuelan government; he promised to govern efficiently with a mere eleven ministries, or at most a dozen. Initially he did reduce the number to fourteen, but by 2008 there were twenty-eight. Chávez has exponentially increased the number of other governmental offices as well. It is extremely difficult to count ministries and ministers, since Chávez deliberately obfuscates them. The Ministry of Energy and Mines becomes the Ministry of Mines and Hydrocarbons; the Ministry of Public Works becomes the Ministry of Urban Planning; the Ministry of Sports and Health becomes the Ministry of Sports Science and Education; and so on. Recent reports list the numbers of Chávez's ministers at a whopping 140.[56] (This does not mean that there have been 140 different people appointed ministers, for Chávez frequently rotates many of his friends through different ministerial positions.)

The credentials for holding an office in Chávez's government seem as arbitrary and corrupt as they ever were. Francis Terán, an aerobics instructor, was appointed president of the National Sports Institute (and, simultaneously, deputy minister of sports) on the basis of her friendship with First Lady Marisabel. Terán, who gave interviews in 2006 detailing how she provided massages to the Great Leader to help him relieve his stress, now advertises her services as a personal trainer on the Internet. Judging by the area code of the phone number she lists on her website, it seems that the former revolutionary/masseuse is now enjoying life in Hawaii.[57]

Chávez's acolytes seem never to doubt his word, for they do not even mention his monumental failure to control the crime problem in Venezuela, nor do they utter a whisper about the other scandalous failures of the Bolivarian Revolution. With stunning illogic, they reason as follows: Chávez claims that crime is down, ergo crime is down; Chávez claims that education has improved, ergo education has improved; Chávez claims that corruption has diminished, ergo corruption has diminished. And anyone who questions these claims or criticizes Chávez is a fascist or a right-wing monster, or simply trash.

A Life of Conspiracies and Lies

That Chávez holds democratic institutions, and indeed many basic aspects of civilized life, in low regard is easy to demonstrate. Virtually all of his adult life has been devoted to the destruction of such institutions. Chávez created his own "revolutionary armed group" as early as 1977, when he was twenty-three.[58] In the years that followed, his conspiratorial impulses continued to evolve, as one revolutionary movement morphed into another and another. Often the movement changed little but its name: The Liberation Army of the Venezuelan People (ELPV) became the Liberation and Revolution 200 movement (LR-200), which later became the Bolivarian Army 200 (EB-200). EB-200 had ties to the Revolution 1983 (R-83) and the Bolivarian

Revolutionary Army 200 (EBR-200), which then became the Bolivarian Revolutionary Movement 200 (MBR-200), then the Bolivarian Revolutionary Movement 2000 (MBR-2000), which for the 1998 elections was changed to the Fifth Republic Movement (MVR). It has recently been eliminated, by decree of the Great Leader, in favor of the United Socialist Party of Venezuela (PSUV).

Words like "army," "revolution," and "liberation" are the expected jargon of young conspirators. The number 200 is a reference to the two-hundredth anniversary of Bolívar's birth, which took place in 1983. After that year, Chávez and his co-conspirators decided that it was silly to keep referring back to 1983, and instead began invoking the year 2000, in tune with millennialism.

The capricious alterations in the names of these conspiratorial groups are reminiscent of the famous scene about revolutionaries in Judea in Monty Python's *Life of Brian* and parts of Woody Allen's *Bananas*. Chávez himself gets confused when talking about these groups; it is hard even for him to keep track of which organization came into existence first and when it morphed into another.[59] Yet the damage that Chávez has caused to his country, and the danger that he continues to represent for Venezuela and the rest of the civilized world, are too real for us merely to laugh at the Chávez-playing-revolutionary charade.

Chávez sees the world in completely Manichean terms: There are only bad guys and good guys, oppressors and oppressed, traitors and patriots. This tendency to turn everything into a simple dichotomy leads to grotesque distortions and exaggerations. Consider the title of Chávez's first insurrectional movement: an army devoted to liberating the Venezuelan people. What exactly were the Venezuelan people being liberated from? As we have seen in the preceding pages, in spite of its many problems, Venezuela's political regime was not one from which people needed to be liberated. Moreover, whatever liberation needed to occur was not the kind that called for an armed rebellion.

In addition, Chávez has a rather corny histrionic side that is a staple of his frequent public appearances. Most of his official acts are surrounded by pomp and circumstance. He loves uniforms and the accoutrements of power, and he recites clichés in the manner of incantations. When he founded his MBR-200, he asked his co-conspirators to join him in taking an oath in front of the Saman de Guere, a tree that is famous in Venezuelan history, some eighty miles west of Caracas.

A type of rain tree, the Saman de Guere has been the subject of various mythological fantasies. Bolívar is said to have rested under its shade before the Battle of Carabobo, arguably the most important victory in his checkered efforts to gain independence from Spain. The oath that Chávez chose was none other than the one that Bolívar, himself no stranger to histrionics and self-aggrandizement, is said to have made during his Italian sojourn: "I swear before you, I swear by the God of my fathers, I swear by my fathers, I swear by my honour, I swear by my country that I will not rest body or soul until I have broken the Spanish chains with which Spain oppresses us."[60] As John Lynch points out, the specific wording of the vow is the subject of some dispute, insofar as it "was reconstructed years later from memory by [Simón] Rodríguez."[61] But no matter. With these words, Chávez vowed to liberate the Venezuelan people—not from Spanish chains, but from the only period of political stability and socioeconomic progress in the country's history.

Chávez's messianic mission led him and his diverse revolutionary groups to plan coups against Venezuela's legitimate governments. These plans took years to develop; as Chávez himself tells us, they organized five "National Congresses" in which the details of armed revolution were discussed.[62] It is shocking that his superiors, particularly those respectful of democratic institutions, would have been so inert in the face of these conspirators. But really, what can one expect of officers some of whom were admitted into the Military Academy because they were good at sports? There were, to be sure, many instances in which Chávez was either detained, or relocated to this or that military bastion, in order to thwart his revolutionary plans. Too little was done, however. No one in the military really took the threat that Chávez represented seriously enough—just as too few Venezuelans took this threat seriously when they elected him president in 1998.

The facts about Chávez's engagement in conspiracy since the beginning of his adult life add to a clear picture of this power-hungry and dishonest man. These facts also highlight a lie that he often repeats—as do his fans abroad even more. His childhood friends claim that since his early years he swore that one day he would be the supreme ruler of Venezuela. But when reporters asked Chávez in 1999 if he had ever imagined that he would be Venezuela's president, he replied "No, never. Never."[63] And this was far from the only time he has made such an assertion.

In his mythologized autobiography, what led him to conspire against Venezuela's legitimate government was one specific incident. On February 27, 1989, during Carlos Andrés Pérez's second government, there was a popular uprising in reaction to a series of probably sensible but poorly explained economic measures imposed by Pérez. The episode is now widely known as the "Caracazo," although it took place in most of Venezuela's large cities, not only in Caracas. The most significant grievance was that Pérez had increased the price of gas, which, while still the cheapest in the world (about ten cents a gallon), affected the cost of many other products and services. Looting was rampant, and the country really was in chaos. Pérez was forced to call in the armed forces to keep order, and he suspended a series of constitutional guarantees regarding the detention of suspects. (The 1961 Constitution had provided for such a suspension in times of emergency.)

As one would imagine, given the violent ways of Venezuelans both inside and outside the armed forces, there were casualties. The number varies widely, depending on the source. The official figure given at the time stood at around 277, though later it was revised upwards by about a hundred. Chavistas tend to claim that the number was more than 3,000, and in some cases at least 10,000.[64] The Inter-American Court of Human Rights, in a decision rendered on November 11,

1999, condemned the Venezuelan government for a series of human rights violations, but recognized only thirty-eight casualties.[65] Still, Chávez panegyrists bombastically refer to the Caracazo as a massacre and as the reason why Chávez decided to lead his own bloody coup in 1992.

Charles Hardy's *Cowboy in Caracas,* for example, depicts widespread killings and mistakenly claims that "constitutional rights had ... been suspended,"[66] when in fact only a smallish subset of such rights were suspended, and this was permitted by the 1961 Constitution (just like Chávez's own Bolivarian one). A chapter in Richard Gott's *Hugo Chávez and the Bolivarian Revolution* is titled "February 1989: Rebellion in Caracas, the Caracazo," which is a rather misleading euphemism for the chaotic looting that afflicted the country during those days.[67] In his *¡Hugo!,* Bart Jones has a chapter devoted to the Caracazo titled "The Massacre." This is followed by "Waiting in the Wings" and "Rebellion of the Angels," which portray Chávez as a veritable messiah who, despite his peaceful nature, was forced to use violence in order to protect innocent people.[68]

In the popular imagination, so systematically manipulated by Chávez, his regime, and his panegyrists, the "massacre" of February 1989 was the reason for the "rebellion" of 1992. These terms are not only inaccurate, but also clearly contradictory to Chávez's own account of his life as a professional conspirator.

Conspiracies, for Chávez, were valuable in and of themselves. In 1995, Agustín Blanco Muñoz asked Chávez if, when he and his comrades began conspiring, they had any idea what would happen if they succeeded in seizing power. Unabashedly, Chávez responded that it was hard for him to answer the question, since the conspiracy had begun so many years ago. He nonetheless admitted that he had no clear goal in mind apart from seizing power. "We only knew we wanted something new," he added.[69]

Chávez did attempt to seize power, by force, on February 4, 1992. The coup had been fastidiously planned for months, and in fact had been on the verge of being carried out at least a couple of times before. Many of the details we know from Chávez himself, who refers to them frequently during his endless speeches and media appearances. The most significant of these declarations may be those made before Chávez was elected. Indeed, he spoke openly about the coup before he ran for president in 1998—and the sordid details of his perfidy did not prevent him from winning by a wide margin. For example, he admitted that the conspirators discussed at length whether or not to assassinate Carlos Andrés Pérez, the legitimate president of Venezuela. Chávez claims that he was against the assassination plot, but neither Chávez nor the millions of Venezuelans who voted for him seemed to see anything unacceptable in the talk of assassination.

The coup was a failure. In spite of many years of preparation, it had been organized haphazardly. Of all the main leaders of the coup, Chávez had the worst performance. Other lieutenant colonels, like Francisco Arias Cárdenas in the oil-rich state of Zulia, succeeded in their missions, but Chávez failed. He was supposed to take over the presidential palace in Caracas; instead he sought refuge in the Museum of Military History a few blocks from the palace and remained there, stationary and ineffectual, for a few hours before eventually surrendering. Members of the opposition, including some of the many who supported Chávez's coup in 1992 but have since abandoned him, refer to Chávez sarcastically as the "Hero of the Military History Museum."

Another important reason the coup failed is that it had no popular support. During the years between the coup and his election, Chávez openly admitted to this;[70] but in recent years, as his megalomania grows, his preferred version is that the masses decisively, overwhelmingly supported him. For example, he now maintains that had the people not supported his coup in 1992, he would not have become president.[71] In fact, it would have been difficult for anyone to support the coup, if only because very few people—only a handful of conspirators—knew about it. Even as it was unfolding, people had no clear idea what was happening until, shortly before the legitimate president addressed the nation, a handful of tanks clumsily climbed the stairs of the presidential palace in downtown Caracas. For most Venezuelans, i.e. those born after 1958, this was a shocking scene: it was the first time they had seen military activity on the streets of their cities. (Not that it was the first time they had seen military *equipment* on the streets, since military parades were always well attended.) All in all, the best way to characterize the reaction of the Venezuelan people is to say that they were utterly stunned.

According to official estimates, the coup caused fourteen deaths, fifty-four wounded, and 1,089 military personnel detained. Other estimates are much higher, calculating more than fifty deaths and more than a hundred wounded.[72] What remains beyond dispute is that all the blood spilled was the result of Chávez's obsession with seizing power. The obsession did not abate while he was in prison awaiting trial.

On November 27, 1992, Venezuelans were the victims of yet another coup, and once again the coup had to a great extent been planned by Chávez, from his prison cell. During an interview in January 1996, Chávez boasted that the video broadcast from the state-owned Venezolana de Televisión station by the November coup leaders had been filmed in his cell.[73] In the November coup, unlike the February 27 coup, the plotters had support in the four forces of the Venezuelan military and in some civilian circles such as the ultra-left Bandera Roja (Red Flag) party. But this coup, too, was poorly organized and lacked sufficient popular support.

Over a hundred members of the Venezuelan armed forces who had led the November coup fled the country and were granted asylum in Peru, under the government of Alberto Fujimori.[74] The choice of Peru is understandable, since Venezuela had broken ties with the country in April of that year in protest of Fujimori's famous self-coup. Venezuela was then still at the forefront in the defense of democracy in Latin America. The coups were clearly antidemocratic in their aims, but Chávez's regime has nevertheless ensured that both be officially celebrated as national holidays.[75]

Paradoxically, perhaps, while neither of Chávez's coup attempts found popular support, Chávez himself began to acquire popular backing immediately after the February coup. This support has been attributed mainly to a brief intervention by Chávez on the occasion of his surrender.[76] Upon capturing him, loyal forces asked Chávez to address the nation and announce his surrender. They thought, somewhat sensibly, that a message from the leader of the coup would help placate the remaining loci of violence in the country. In the event, however, it was foolish to give Chávez a chance to speak to the nation *live*. He babbled about the Bolivarian message that he was "throwing" to the nation. Then he asked his comrades to surrender, but he explained that the reason for this surrender was that *por ahora* ("for now") the goals had not been achieved, and that "the future will bring better things." The words *por ahora* became a veritable rallying cry, which ignited the easily inflamed Venezuelan imagination.

Venezuelans were deeply dissatisfied with their previous regimes and were eager for change. I would dare suggest that they were too eager, for they embraced a confessed, proud, recidivist felon, and made him president. Admittedly, many of those who supported Chávez, including some of his closest allies, have come to detest him. Alas, it is now too late; for he has a firm grip on power, and it is hard to imagine him ever handing it over peacefully.

In 1994, less than two years after Chávez orchestrated his second coup, President Rafael Caldera released him from prison. As noted above, this did not constitute a pardon, for Caldera released Chávez before there had been a trial. Had he waited until Chávez had been convicted and then pardoned him, Chávez would have been ineligible to run for president. It has been unpersuasively argued—by one of Caldera's sons, for instance—that the release of Chávez is excusable because it was desired by broad segments of the public, as well as by the Venezuelan intelligentsia.[77] In fact, that public sympathy epitomizes the general decay of civic culture in Venezuela.[78] Moreover, Caldera did not merely release the conspirators; he rewarded them with nice jobs. Francisco Arias Cárdenas, Chávez's number-two man, was put in charge of the Food Program for Mothers and Infants; Jesús Urdaneta Hernández was named Venezuelan consul in Vigo, Spain; Joel Acosta Chirinos was "offered a job at the communications ministry," and so on.[79] This is how justice looks in the Caribbean.

Andrés Oppenheimer saw a dispiriting combination of passivity and opportunism in Venezuela at the time:

> What impressed me the most on my trip to Venezuela after the attempted coup in 1992 was the passivity—almost complacency—with which the majority of Venezuelans reacted to the attempted coup. Those of us who had seen the military dictatorships of the sixties in South America were horrified by what had just happened. Venezuela was one of the oldest democracies in Latin America, where the last military regime had ended in 1959 [sic]. And instead of repudiating the bloody coup, many Venezuelans would shrug their shoulders, or would say that the government deserved it. In my room at the Caracas Hilton, watching the televised session of the Venezuelan Congress in which the events of the last few hours were being discussed, I was struck by how the legislators—who in theory should have been at the forefront in the defense of democracy—gave firebrand speeches criticizing the president of Venezuela, rather than putting aside their own partisan differences in order to condemn the coup. The former president and by then the opposition senator, Rafael Caldera, with an opportunism that made me grab my head in indignation, demanded that the Congress should "rectify the economic policies of the government." ... A short while later [Caldera] was asking for Pérez's resignation. Populism and insincerity seem to run in the blood of Venezuelan politics of all tendencies.[80]

It is beyond the scope of this book to attempt an etiology of Venezuela's political myopia. The question transcends Venezuela: many nations, including better educated and more advanced ones, have elected incompetent, even criminal presidents. Two factors at work in Chávez's success were the overall messianic view of politics in Venezuela (and in Latin America), and what was perhaps the worst shortcoming of Venezuelan democracy: the impoverished educational system.

Easy Victories Follow Cheap Pardons

Soon after Chávez's coup attempt, Venezuelans, perhaps following the lead of their opportunistic politicians, began to call for his pardon. They appealed to two interrelated arguments in order to lend weight to this strange request: first, that the legitimate government was terribly corrupt, and second, that Chávez had been driven to the use of force by love for his country. That what Chávez had done was not only illegal but also immoral, catapulting Venezuela back to its incredibly unstable past, was lost on the great majority of Venezuelans.

While still in jail, Chávez became a sort of iconic figure. People from all walks of life sought his company and offered him advice and help. This crass indulgence helps explain Chávez's swift road to stardom after he was released from prison. He immediately recommended various anti-establishment measures and vehemently refused to participate in anything resembling democratic elections. Initially, he urged people to abstain from voting in any election; later on, he toned down his rhetoric just a bit, claiming that "in this moment in history there is no way [of attaining power] that can be discarded."[81] It seems that for Chávez, "this moment in history" referred to any moment during his lifetime. In any case, he never denied that he would use violent means again.

A few months later, however, Chávez took a new tack: He was running for president, as it had become apparent to him that this was a faster and easier route to power. He underwent a major transformation in his attire, exchanging his fatigues and army boots for Armani suits and Gucci shoes. But he also altered the most strident aspects of his earlier rhetoric: Now he was a friend of foreign investors, of private property, and of Western values in general. Banking on the relative popularity of Tony Blair's "third way" at the time, he proclaimed himself to be "the Tony Blair of the Caribbean." While he did not renounce violent means, he did promise that he would resign the presidency if and whenever the people asked him to do so, insisting that he had no desire to remain in power. In fact, he claimed not even to have desired power in the first place; he was but a small cog in the deterministic machinery of history. When journalists asked him what he would do if he lost the election, Chávez, unflappable, simply insisted that this option was "not conceivable." In other words, he could lose *only* if the old regime meddled somehow, in which case he would lead the masses into a bloodbath.

But the essence of Chávez's views remained the same Manichean and narcissistic mess they had been all along: Everything that the previous governments of Venezuela had done was bad, and there was only one solution to the nation's woes: Chávez himself. In fact, even with his toned-down persona during the presidential campaign, when he turned into a devout and humble family man, he would not abjure violence. As he defended his main campaign argument, a proposal to convene a National Constituent Assembly for the purpose of writing a new constitution, he unequivocally stated that this proposal was "a process that has nothing to do with the elites; it comes from below, from the very people. It is a revolutionary process which seeks to destroy this [democratic] system; unlike other projects, ours does not seek to fix this system."[82]

Chávez's indifference to civilized procedures was also perfectly obvious before he became president. Agustín Blanco Muñoz once asked him whether participating in elections was an appropriate way to achieve what Chávez glibly called "a new ethical system for the new Venezuelan." (The implications of this shopworn talk of a "new ethics" for a "new man" seem not to have caught the attention of enough Venezuelans.) Chávez replied by saying that "any way, be it electoral, military, dressing up as priests, looking like Christ, or invoking the Moon sect, is doubtful, because there is nothing exact in the human being. We all have both God and the devil inside."[83] In other words, establishing the new morality necessarily went through his seizing of power, and if all ways of attaining power were "doubtful," any way was acceptable.

Moreover, Chávez displayed the same sort of verbal incontinence for which he is notorious. Consider his reflections after Blanco Muñoz asked him whether he was afraid to be called violent:

> No, we do not have any fear. Moreover, not too long ago we were invited to the closing of the World Congress on Violence '98, and I spoke there, and I said it: The son of violence? Yes, I am, because I think that violence is natural to the human being, and to the universe itself. A very weighty scientific current speaks about the fact that the origin of everything is that explosion [the Big Bang, one assumes]. A meteorite is about to pass close to earth and threatens our existence, that is violence. A volcano, the phenomenon of El Niño, nature itself is filled with violence. We are the children of this nature. Cain and Abel, so many wars, violence and more violence. Now, the issue is that as I said in my speech there, often the violence of the downtrodden is just, when it is directed against that other violence which negates life. It is a defensive violence, to defend the right to exist, the right to life, the right to be. Thus, I have no fear whatsoever, nor do I go around making exorcisms so as to be seen now with flowers. I am the son of a violent process. He who says that he lives in a process or a world of peace, that I am the harmony, the smile, that those others are the violent ones and I am the peace, that simply is cynicism, because we are all loaded with violence.[84]

And on and on. Yet Venezuelans still voted for this charlatan by a wide margin.

Perhaps the greatest sign of decadence in the traditional parties in Venezuela was their behavior in the elections of 1998, when Chávez was made president. In the previous elections, Caldera had significantly weakened COPEI, the party of Christian democrats that he himself had founded. Somewhat clueless in the absence of its own great leader, COPEI chose to nominate Irene Sáez, a former Miss Universe who had been the mayor of Chacao, an affluent neighborhood in Caracas. The choice was initially well received by the Christian democrats, and early in the campaign Sáez was ahead in most polls. But campaigning quickly wore her down, and she plummeted in the polls even more quickly than she had climbed them. The formerly glorious AD (Democratic Action) nominated Luis Alfaro Ucero, the ultimate apparatchik: an almost senile man with virtually no charisma or education (not that Sáez was much better educated). With these choices, the parties turned against their own young potential candidates, and against the population at large, both of whom clamored for change.

There was a third candidate, Henrique Salas Römer, a pseudo-independent whose origins are to be found in COPEI. A Yale graduate, Salas had been a well-liked governor in the important industrial state of Carabobo, and he enjoyed some popular support. But he appeared somewhat stodgy and distant. Chávez, appealing to the electorate's baser emotions, effectively ridiculed Salas throughout the campaign. Mere days before Election Day, AD and COPEI, certain that their candidates had no chance, turned their backs on them and instead supported Salas Römer. This cynical move was too little too late, and it was insulting not only to the candidates they had chosen initially, but also to the electorate itself. Moreover, this move may have strengthened Chávez's candidacy in a number of ways. He suddenly seemed to be singlehandedly facing all the other parties combined.

There is no disputing that Chávez skillfully exploited his instant status as yet another messiah in Venezuela's long line of saviors, or that this status was, above all, due to Venezuela's political immaturity. The country transformed him into a hero simply because he broke the law. But it would be difficult to dispute the idea that the traditional political parties made things easier for him. Had at least one of the parties presented a credible candidate, it is unlikely that he would have won the presidency so easily, if at all. Chávez won with roughly 56 percent of the vote, against the roughly 40 percent that went to Salas Römer. The initial candidates of the traditional parties together got less than 4 percent of the vote: slightly under 3 percent went to Sáez and slightly under 0.5 percent to Alfaro Ucero.[85]

Interestingly, while the social democrats (AD) got only 0.4 percent of the vote for president, they won a hefty 35.2 percent of the votes for Congress—more than any other party. The Christian democrats (COPEI) also did better at the congressional level: while they obtained less than 3 percent for president, they got 13 percent for Congress. Parties opposing Chávez won a majority not only in Congress, but also in gubernatorial positions. And yet, just as they proved inept in preventing Chávez's victory at the elections, the opposition eventually proved itself incapable of preventing Chávez's assault on democratic institutions after he was elected. A couple of years later, the opposition went as far as throwing its support behind Francisco Arias Cárdenas, one of Chávez's main co-conspirators.

Chávez's (Eternal and Omnipotent) Presidency

According to Venezuelan law, while Chávez was elected president on December 6, 1998, he was not actually to take power until February 2, 1999. In the interval, he began to change and ignore some of Venezuela's political traditions. For example, instead of living in his own residence until the appointed time to move into the presidential mansion, Chávez "demanded to move into La Viñeta, a residence for state visitors within the Fort Tiuna military complex," Caracas's most important military base. His wish was granted. Once at La Viñeta, Chávez frequently hosted ostentatious parties, with "fun and games for him and his friends."[86] This extravagance continued through his inauguration. While some previous inaugurations in Venezuela were very opulent—for instance, that of Carlos Andrés Pérez in 1989—Chávez's is widely considered "the most expensive Venezuela has ever seen."[87]

Chávez's conspicuous consumption is also on display in his travels. During his six weeks as president-elect, he visited twelve countries—more than any previous Venezuelan president-elect. As the BBC reported, during his first 808 days in power, Chávez had spent 119 days abroad;[88] during his first 1,095 days in office, he was abroad 170 days.[89] The only thing that has changed in this pattern is the countries he visits. In the beginning, he visited the United States and Western European countries; his travels have become progressively more focused on Iraq, Iran, Libya, Belarus, Russia, Bolivia, Argentina, and especially Cuba.

There is extravagance, too, in the opulent style in which Chávez travels. In a move that drew considerable criticism from Venezuelans, he bought a new presidential airplane. (The old presidential plane was used to take Marisabel and her kids to Disney World; after Chávez and Marisabel were divorced, it was mostly used to give rides to Chávez's friends.) He had two requirements for this plane, which Venezuelans dubbed "Chupadolares," the "dollar-guzzler": that it be extremely luxurious and that it not be built in the United States.[90] Chávez and his retinue stay at the most expensive suites in the most expensive hotels wherever they go. His entourage is typically immense—usually numbering in the hundreds, including masseuses, cooks, tailors, and a team of Cuban doctors. On more than one occasion, it has included Helena Ibarra, a Venezuelan fashionista who went from being manager of Venezuela's most famous punk-rock band (Sentimiento Muerto) to being a reputed chef, whose job during these trips was "to supervise the cocktails for the Chávez delegation."[91]

A pattern of big spending is visible not only in Chávez and his immediate relatives and entourage, but also in many other mid- to high-level functionaries. These "revolutionaries" are typically seen in Caracas and other cities driving luxurious cars: the traditional Mercedes Benz or the new vehicle of choice, the Hummer. Chávez, his relatives, and his chums sport expensive designer clothes and jewelry while they indulge in an exuberant lifestyle.

This description of Chávez's outrageous spending foregrounds the disconnect between his speech and his deeds. His discourse is preoccupied with frugality and modesty. He has accused Venezuelans of being immature and materialistic, of spending too much money. He has specifically asserted that "to be well-off is a bad thing,"[92] and has suggested that those who want to have money should leave the country.[93] Meanwhile, he continues to live large, spending Venezuelans' money at a pace never before seen in any of his predecessors. In July 2008, as he visited Russia to buy yet more weapons, a boastful Chávez told the Russians: "Do not worry about where to get the money [to buy] missiles of short, medium, and *looooong* range, because I can take care of the money."[94] His many acolytes in the United States and elsewhere seem unconcerned about Chávez's bellicose spending spree—or about the ways his regime tramples on democratic institutions.

The regime has been characterized by a reactionary concentration of power in one man, by a concomitant infringement on individual liberties, and by harassment of anything resembling an opposition. Among the few campaign promises that Chávez has kept is his call for a National Constituent Assembly to draft a new constitution to replace the "moribund" 1961 Constitution—Venezuela's longest-lasting constitution, which he had sworn to uphold. Venezuela before Chávez did have major problems: corruption, criminality, and economic trouble. But these are not constitutional matters, and the very idea that they could be resolved by enacting a new constitution is absurd.

Since Chávez did not have the majority in Congress, and since it was clear that the majority in Congress would oppose the Constituent Assembly as he envisioned it, he circumvented Congress altogether by holding a referendum. The Venezuelan people, still intoxicated by Chávez's recent victory and indifferent to the Congress, voted in favor of a constitutional assembly by 87.75 percent. True, the abstention rate was 62.35 percent, but this was nevertheless a landslide victory (again, speaking volumes about the ineptitude of the opposition in Venezuela and the general political myopia of the populace).[95]

On the heels of this victory, Chávez packed the Constituent Assembly with his supporters. Opposition members were represented only in symbolic fashion: of the 128 members of the assembly, only eight belonged to the opposition. But there was something else particularly alarming about the assembly: It was supposed to stand *above* the normal branches of the government—above the Supreme Court, the Congress, and everything else. It was accountable to no individual or institution. In Chávez's own words, it was "supra-constitutional."[96] In effect, it was a coup d'état. There was no more division of power or checks and balances in the Venezuelan government.

Of course, there was an exception to the claim that the Constituent Assembly was accountable to no one: it was not merely accountable to Chávez but under his direct control. For example, he gave it a draft constitution that he himself had written to use as a "blueprint." The resulting Bolivarian Constitution contained pretty much everything Chávez had demanded. It did not break any new ground regarding individual liberties. What it did was to concentrate power in the president, and it changed the name of the country to one that Chávez liked: the Bolivarian Republic of Venezuela. (Imagine the Washingtonian United States of America.) It extended the term of the president from five to six years and introduced the possibility for an immediate reelection of the sitting president.

These "innovations" are by now easily understood as the result of Chávez's anachronistic endorsements of Bolívar's ideas, which were suspect and mostly obsolete in the early nineteenth century. But Chávez's reelection scheme deserves more attention. As we saw above, although Chávez had claimed that his constitution would last a thousand years, he suggested in 2007 that it stood in need of a major overhaul. And so he campaigned for another new constitution. Aside from his characteristic attempts to grant himself more and more power, the most noteworthy modification of this newest constitution was that it would allow him to remain in power indefinitely, via unlimited reelections. In a transparent attempt to persuade the populace to vote for his proposal, Chávez offered to reduce the work week from forty to thirty-six hours. Still, he narrowly lost the referendum, held on December 2, 2007. (As of July 2008, in spite of many requests by the opposition, Chávez's Electoral Council had refused to disclose the official results, arguing that they are irrelevant, since Chávez admitted defeat.)

Chávez's reaction to this defeat was predictable. First, in his usual vulgar fashion, he called the opposition's victory a *victoria de mierda* ("a victory of shit").[97] It is difficult to impress upon non-Spanish speakers how Chávez's very pronunciation is vulgar. There is a way of pronouncing words, a sort of guttural tinge, that renders a vulgar word even more so, and this is exactly what Chávez does: So *mierda* becomes *"mieeehhhrrrda,"* which sounds much worse.

Second, in his "concession" speech, Chávez suggested that the margin by which he had supposedly lost was so small that he could appeal the results and perhaps end up winning. Yet Chávez, full of grace, in his infinite generosity, decided to let the opposition have this "Pyrrhic" victory. (He misused the word "Pyrrhic," of course, taking it to mean "close" when it actually means "costly.") He shamelessly implied that the opposition's victory was his own gracious gift, saying that he had faced a "great dilemma"—whether or not to recognize defeat—before he decided to address the nation and present his gift to the opposition.[98]

In spite of this obvious affront to the rule of law, many people thought his concession showed that Chávez is indeed a champion of democracy and the accusation that he is a dictator but a tissue of lies. Chávez himself spun his defeat in the referendum of 2007 into the idea that he is a champion of democracy, but this is hardly credible. And many of his supporters soon began to discuss loopholes and odd interpretations of Venezuelan law that would allow the proposal for indefinite reelection to be considered again. Moreover, on July 31, 2008, by way of an Orwellian "enabling law" that allows him to legislate in all sorts of areas, Chávez smuggled into currency many of the provisions that were defeated in the constitutional referendum of 2007. On the very last day of validity of his latest enabling law, Chávez passed, by decree, twenty-six laws ranging from tourism and *soberania agroalimentaria* ("agricultural and food-related sovereignty") to the dramatic erosion of private property (he can expropriate anything Venezuelans own without so much as a legal proceeding) and the creation of new armed forces.

The new "Bolivarian Armed Forces" are directly and exclusively under the command of Chávez, who has invented a rank just for himself. He has sole discretion and authority in matters relating to budget, promotion, expulsion, and so on. The structure of parts of Chávez's Bolivarian armed forces seems to have been inspired by Hitler's Schutzstaffel, known in the annals of infamy as the SS. Like the SS, Chávez's newly created National Bolivarian Militia is accountable only to him personally; it is a paramilitary force that mysteriously "complements" the regular army, as stated in Article 43 of the Law of the Bolivarian Armed Forces.[99]

Chávez's new laws are adorned with predictable boilerplate such as "we need to ensure the rebirth of a new citizenry, and a new citizen … in our road to a new socialist society."[100] But these laws violate a central principle of any civilized government: that matters belonging to tax and criminal law are such that the legislative branch of government cannot delegate them. In other words, no enabling law can create new taxes or new crimes. This is one of the essential strengths of the division of pow ers: to ensure that decisions pertaining to matters that affect individuals so dramatically are never made by a single person. Chávez's new laws *do* create new taxes and new crimes, and they even deny the usual defense procedures to the victims of these regulations.

For example, Section VII of the Law for the Defense of Persons in Access to Goods and Services is titled "Of Crimes and Punishments." True to its title, the section contains a slew of newly created crimes, such as:

> Article 139: Those who alone or in conjunction with others, develop or carry out actions, or omissions, which may hinder, directly or indirectly, the production, manufacture, import, recollection, transportation, distribution, and merchandising of goods deemed [by the Great Leader] basic, will be punished with prison terms of six to ten years.[101]

The law also penalizes "generic usury" with prison. Usury is defined as "acquiring an advantage, directly or indirectly," which might be deemed (again, by the Great Leader) to be "notoriously disproportionate to the effort put into the operation."[102] Thus, if someone is really smart and enters into a deal in which he does very well without having made much of an effort, he could be convicted under Chávez's law. As if this were not enough, Chávez creates a new, expedited, and abusive procedure to prosecute and punish these crimes; for example, the documents used against a person can be kept secret at Chávez's sole discretion if he deems it necessary (i.e., if he feels like it).[103] The twenty-six new laws, moreover, provide for further clarification and fine-tuning over the course of time, so Chávez can change them at will. This provision renders the "end" of the enabling law rather pointless.

There are many more instances of this outrageous abuse of power. The fact that these laws and decrees violate the very Bolivarian Constitution that Chávez passed a few years back with great fanfare seems to be of no consequence to international commentators. Also of no special interest, it seems, is the fact that many of these laws reproduce the measures that Chávez sought (and failed) to impose by constitutional "reform." Sure, the opposition in Venezuela has rightly complained about all these abuses and illegalities. Even Luis Miquilena, once Chávez's right-hand man and "ideological father" (as Chávez described him), has called the laws of July 31, 2008, a veritable coup d'état.[104] But few outside Venezuela seem to be listening.

Chávez's original term ended in February 2004. He has doubled the term that he was supposed to spend in office—something expressly prohibited by the constitution under which he was elected. In a pathetic display of subservience to the Great Leader, Chávez's Supreme Court (filled with his chums, of course) decided that the first two years of his term did not count. Their "reasoning" was as follows: Insofar as Venezuela ceased to be Venezuela in the year 2000, when it became the Bolivarian Republic of Venezuela, the first two years of Chávez's presidency amounted to a term as president of another country. Thus, by enacting a new constitution, Chávez was *ipso facto* elected for a fresh new "first" term.

In December of 2008, Chávez formally announced a new effort to amend the constitution so as to allow himself to stay in power indefinitely.

Mere hours after this announcement, the National Assembly meekly rubber-stamped the Great Leader's proposal to conduct a referendum on amending the constitution. On February 15, 2009, Chávez won this referendum, and thus he is now allowed to run for president in perpetuity. He has repeatedly asserted that he is the only person capable of ruling Venezuela.

Some believe that insofar as Chávez did consult the Venezuelan people about the Constituent Assembly that produced the Bolivarian Constitution, insofar as the Venezuelan people did vote for it, insofar as Chávez recognized defeat when he lost an election and then submitted to a new referendum, he has done everything in a perfectly democratic way. But this position is naïve, at best. First of all, democracy is not simply a matter of voting. A ruler could be democratically elected and yet not rule democratically—just think of Hitler or Saddam Hussein, who used to win elections with virtually 100 percent of the vote (the percentage with which Chávez won the congressional elections of 2005, for example). Second, the ways in which elections have been conducted in Venezuela since Chávez took over are clearly unfair.[105] He has access to all the media, with no limits whatsoever, and to all the money one could possibly imagine. He systematically harasses the opposition. For the regional elections of November 2008, for example, his regime arbitrarily declared almost four hundred Venezuelans ineligible for office.[106] (Coincidentally, many of these individuals, according to polls, had a better chance to win in these elections—what a surprise!) And all these obvious irregularities are in addition to the allegations of fraud that serious scholars have raised against some of the previous elections Chávez has held.[107]

Chávez has sought to rebuild Venezuela from the ground up, entirely in accordance with his own preferences. The extent to which his caprices become law is truly astonishing. For example, on March 12, 2006, he chose to change the Seal of Venezuela. The white horse depicted running toward the right would now run toward the left. Why spend a fortune to change this? Why notice it in the first place? Chávez admits that the inspiration came from his nine-year-old daughter, Rosinés. How telling that the whims of a nine-year-old girl become law in Venezuela.

Some of Chávez's bright ideas only *seem* to have come from a nine-year-old. One day he announced that he had noticed, while looking at a world map, that the official time in Venezuela was erroneous—that Venezuela was farther to the east than the official time would suggest. Thus, he ordered that the official time in Venezuela be changed by half an hour. Chávez made the announcement of the new official time on national television—but he did not understand his own proposal very well, for he suggested that the clocks should be moved forward, when in fact they should have been moved backward,[108] as the authorities of Venezuela's Naval Observatory later clarified.[109] Their task was not easy, for they needed to contradict what the Great Leader had said on national television, without mentioning that he had said the exact opposite of what he should have. At any rate, Chávez, as almost always, got his way: Venezuela's official time has been changed for the first time in its history.

Chávez's whims go beyond legislation. He really does whatever he pleases, whenever and wherever he pleases. For example, he sings, and he teaches Venezuelans how to sing; he has even sung during press conferences and in international meetings with other heads of state. He regularly recites poetry, written either by famous poets or by himself, whenever he feels like doing it. At a popular arts and crafts fair in 2006, Chávez congratulated an old lady for her painting of a nature scene. After scrutinizing it for a couple of minutes, he decided that the picture was missing something. He proceeded to grab a brush, on national television, and add a tree in the lower left corner—"for balance," the Great Painter explained.

In fact, Chávez has claimed that he always wanted to be a painter, that painting was his true calling. As with so many other things, it is hard to take him seriously, since he has claimed at other times that his true calling was baseball, physics, mathematics, history, geography, cartography, philosophy, what have you. To an extent, he has been able to fulfill his childhood dreams, for he now sings, recites poetry, teaches mathematics, physics, and economics, corrects official maps of the country, plays baseball (both in Cuba and at Shea Stadium in New York City), announces soccer and baseball, all in front of a captive audience of millions.[110]

Chávez's speeches are a combination of variety show, pseudo-pedagogical multimedia harangue, and disclosure of military plans—both his own and his enemies'. The parallels between Chávez and other Great Leaders, such as Idi Amin, are pronounced. Recently Chávez accused the United States of espionage and of listening to his phone conversations. Jaime Bayly, a perspicuous television anchor from Peru, quipped that it would be unnecessary to spy on Chávez since he spills everything on his mind during his own television show. (Incidentally, in September 2008, Chávez accused Bayly of being part of a conspiracy to assassinate him. With his usual wit, Bayly said that he wasn't involved because he didn't have the spare time.)[111] More to the point, Chávez has boasted that he has "infiltrated the opposition to the bones," and that he can hear everything every member of the opposition in Venezuela says. Of course this is illegal, but no matter. Leading figures of Chávez's government hold press conferences in which they play illegally obtained audio recordings of conversations between Chávez's opponents, and they do this with complete impunity and to the applause of commentators.[112]

Coherence and integrity are unknown to Chávez. Today he says whatever he feels like saying, and tomorrow he will say exactly the opposite, without batting an eye, and utterly free from criticism. Immunity from criticism has turned him into a veritable tropical parrot. Not that he was intellectually rigorous before seizing power, but he would sometimes think before he spoke, if only for strategic reasons. Chávez's malapropisms—reminiscent of the character Slip Mahoney in *The Bowery Boys*—have become incessant. For example, in a recent speech he chided his aides for not studying "epistemology, the philosophical discipline which studies the origin of words." That the word he wanted was "etymology" was of no consequence in Venezuela. No one, even in the opposition, seems to have noticed.

But Chávez's verbal sins can be more serious, like the protracted account of his ordeal with diarrhea that he delivered on national television, not sparing any of the scatological details. The whole nation had to watch and listen as Chávez described trying to contract his sphincter muscles, how the sensation was "like giving birth," and how he desperately scouted for a suitable place "behind some bushes" to have a bowel movement.[113] The court flatterers in attendance at the "press conference," including most members of his always-in-flux cabinet, had to laugh out loud and applaud Chávez's recounting of his *kampf,* never mind that it was a sickening abuse of Venezuelans' money, time, and dignity. Moreover, many of those in his audiences are forced to be there: various official memos have surfaced revealing that public employees are threatened into attending Chávez's press conferences.[114]

Chávez often offends and disgusts his audience, but his loquacity sometimes brings about good things. For example, it is believed that his cell-phone calls to some of his contacts in the Colombian terrorist group FARC (Revolutionary Armed Forces of Colombia) led to the killing or capture of some of them. Some suggest that many of the Colombian government's recent successes in its fight against the terrorists are attributable in part to Chávez's mindless chatter, which has provided useful information as to the whereabouts of terrorists and drug dealers.[115]

I will have more to say in the next chapter about FARC and Chávez's other dangerous friends, for it would be a mistake to regard Chávez as a mere clown, a flamboyant bird from the Caribbean. A clown Chávez most certainly is, but his caprices are not all simply idiotic or innocuous. Chávez is resentful and harbors real hatred against the West in general and the United States in particular. To top it all off, he has money, immense amounts of it. So while many of his projects are carried out in clownish and inefficient ways, they do have consequences, both for Venezuelans and for the world.

CHAPTER THREE

CHÁVEZ'S IMPACT ON VENEZUELANS AND BEYOND

While Chávez's verbal incontinence, his predilection for undemocratic means, and his obsession with power have been visible since he became a recognizable figure in Venezuelan politics, some things changed dramatically after he seized power. One is the civility of political life in Venezuela. During the democratic period that preceded Chávez, being in the opposition was not a major problem for ordinary Venezuelans. Sure, cronyism and corruption have always figured in Venezuelan politics, but there were no major disadvantages to opposition status. By contrast, Chávez has persecuted and in many ways harmed opposition members simply for being in the opposition. He repeatedly claims that whoever is against him is a traitor.

Not for being puerile is this any less dangerous—particularly with a populace that was not well educated to begin with and is now being systematically brainwashed. Lina Ron, a longtime political associate of Chávez, declared on national television that she was willing to kill anyone *voting* against Chávez, or to die in the attempt to prevent someone from voting against the "Messiah of Venezuela."[1]

One of Chávez's favorite phrases, which he began using when he ran for president in 1998 and now repeats constantly, claiming that it "inspires him,"[2] is the Carib motto: *"Ana cariná rote, amucón papóroro itóto mantó."*[3] In English this means: "Only we are people/humans, the rest are only slaves."[4] This abominable expression does capture how Chávez and his followers view political life: they are the only ones who matter; others have no rights.[5] Chávez refers to the opposition as "squalid." Incredibly, this insulting label has stuck in Venezuela and has become a synonym for "opposition."[6] Thus, by definition, those who disagree with Chávez are morally repulsive and filthy. Even those who do not clearly oppose him but happen to ask him an unscripted question have to face his wrath.[7]

Most instances of Chávez's persecution and harassment are, as one would expect, officially denied; after all, what government openly admits to such things? But there are many well-documented examples, including a systematic process of political discrimination and abuse to which, surprisingly, Chávez has admitted.

The Recall Referendum

Soon after Chávez set about dismantling democratic institutions in Venezuela, the opposition began looking for ways to stop him. The Bolivarian Constitution provided for the possibility of a "general referendum," whereby the people could vote on matters of "national significance." Reasonably, the opposition assumed that the potential termination of a president's term of office qualified as a matter of "national significance," and so they embarked on the process of collecting the signatures required for activating such a referendum.

Before becoming president, Chávez had stated repeatedly that if people did not like him, he would simply leave office; yet he put all sorts of impediments in the path of this referendum. In the end, and even though the opposition had collected over four million signatures, almost twice as many as necessary, Chávez's Supreme Court ruled in favor of his argument that the referendum would be illegal because the constitution also provided for a specific "recall referendum," which could take place only after half of the presidential term had been served. Exquisite though indefensible legalese—and this from Chávez, formerly the arch-enemy of legal technicalities—won the day, preventing the Venezuelan people from expressing their opinion.

A year later, in August 2003, the midpoint of the presidential term had passed and so the opposition tried to use the signatures it had collected during the aborted general referendum to activate the recall referendum. Chávez's regime now claimed that the signatures were invalid and that the opposition had to start anew. This time, the regime put up even more hurdles: It severely limited the number of collecting centers, making it virtually impossible for some people to sign the forms; it required that the forms be printed on a special paper of the sort used for bank notes, causing major delays; it deliberately printed too few forms; it sent memos to the immense multitude of public employees threatening them with firing if they voted in favour of the referendum. During the process, Chávez boastfully ridiculed the whole enterprise, saying that he would never leave office "even if the opposition got 90 percent of the vote,"[8] and he intimidated the people by suggesting that they would be "traitors" to vote against him.

A telling demand that Chávez made of Venezuelans who wanted to activate the referendum was that in order to vote they must fill out a form including their full names, their fingerprints, their legal addresses, their ID card numbers (roughly analogous to Social Security numbers in the United States), and their signatures. Thus, the vote was not secret, although Venezuelan law required that it be. Predictably, Chávez's friends at the Supreme Court found an "argument" showing that there was nothing illegal about this mechanism. Even though it was organized and carried out by the National Electoral Council (CNE), and even though people expressed their preferences and these were tallied and compared, the vote was declared to be "not electoral in nature." There were, technically speaking, no "votes." Thus, the constitutional requirement of secrecy did not really apply. And so it went.

In spite of all the obstacles and threats, the opposition went ahead and gathered a second set of signatures in favor of activating a referendum on whether Chávez's term ought to be cut short. In November 2003, over three million signatures were collected—around a million more than were needed. But Chávez's regime was not done; his efforts to derail the referendum involved a new two-pronged strategy. First, he ordered the Electoral Council to give the original forms to him and to one of his assistants, Luis Tascón, a deputy in the National Assembly. This was illegal, yet the CNE promptly handed over the documents, which became the basis for the "Lista Tascón"—to which I will return later. Second, after Chávez revised the forms, the CNE claimed that well over a million of the signatures were of dubious authenticity, and then ordered another collection. (Recall that the members of the CNE were later shown to be close aides to Chávez, who rewarded them with important political posts.)

For a third time, in May 2004, Venezuelans signed, now to verify that the signatures they had given before—accompanied by fingerprints and addresses, printed on special paper—were really theirs. The ratification process that Chávez put in place was delayed endlessly; rules were changed on a daily basis, always in such a way as to make the referendum less likely. Still, and in spite of all the obstacles and the fact that Chávez had already begun firing those who signed in favor of the recall referendum, Venezuelans ratified their signatures yet again and managed to activate the referendum.

The referendum, held on August 15, was as much a morass of immorality and illegality as the process that, against all odds, had somehow led to it. For example, all the millions of Venezuelans who signed in favor of the referendum were prohibited from being witnesses in voting centers, effectively ensuring that all the personnel working at the centers were Chávez's supporters. Chávez won the referendum by an ample margin, with roughly 60 percent of the vote. But this margin of victory was almost exactly what many of the exit polls, carried out by international agencies, had given in favor of the opposition. Thus, the discrepancy between the exit polls and the actual results was roughly 40 points.

Neither this immense discrepancy, nor the tortuous process, nor the obvious instances of cheating, abuse of power, and other irregularities prevented Jimmy Carter or the Organization of American States from swiftly endorsing the results of the referendum (though the OAS was neither as quick nor as happy with the process as was Carter). The strongest condemnation of the situation came from the European Union, which refused to oversee the referendum in light of the mountain of restrictions that the Chávez regime had established.[9] The opposition demanded a manual recount, but Carter was steadfast in opposing it, though he had demanded much more during the disputes in Florida following the presidential election between George W. Bush and Al Gore in 2000. It is not surprising at all that Carter became *persona non grata* to many Venezuelans.

The aftermath of the referendum wreaked havoc on Venezuelans. Thousands upon thousands lost their jobs merely because they or their relatives had signed the petition to activate the referendum. Thousands were denied passports, loans, diplomas from state universities, employment, contracts, pensions, and so on. Chávez conducted a veritable *razzia* with the information he had gathered in the Lista Tascón. Since the list contains the actual addresses of the signatories, there have been countless cases in which his minions have physically injured people who signed in favor of a referendum.[10]

During the months following the referendum, Chávez made fun of the list's signatories on television, intimidating and humiliating them. Almost a year after the referendum, however, and after indignation about the layoffs and other irregularities reached the boiling point, Chávez admitted that the list had outlived its usefulness, that it was time to "bury" it. (Incidentally, he thereby made his many aides who had denied that the list was being used look like fools.) The Lista Tascón has in fact morphed into other lists, such as the Lista Maisanta, the Lista Santa Ines, and the Lista Florentino. A further refinement assigns a numerical value, from one to six, to an individual's opposition to the regime (based on whether he has abstained from voting for Chávez, has actually voted against him, has reconfirmed his "questionable" signature, and so on). I am by no means unique in possessing copies of some of these lists, since they have become such a common item in Venezuela that they are sold by street vendors in broad daylight in Caracas. Printouts are available, but the favored format is digital: You buy a CD or a DVD with all the information of the "squalid" opposition. The price of the list, containing sensitive information about the voting population of Venezuela, is around two dollars.

The Tenor of Public Discourse

Just as the physical integrity, the livelihood, the freedom of movement of many Venezuelans who oppose Chávez has suffered, the very sanity of all Venezuelans—whether Chavistas or not—has also been threatened. For something else that has changed since Chávez seized power is his language and his demeanor, and with this change the general level of political discourse in Venezuela has plummeted. Before Chávez, it was customary for presidential candidates to conduct live televised debates in which, as elsewhere in the civilized world, they would discuss and defend their ideas and projects. This came to an abrupt halt after Chávez seized power. He has refused to debate any opposition candidate; asserting that "eagles do not hunt flies," an allusion to his supposed stature among the "dwarfs," "fags," "limp-dicks," and "squealing pigs" who oppose him. In a Kafkaesque move, however, he boasts that he, unlike his opponents, relishes debate. Apparently he doesn't know the difference between a debate and a monologue.

Chávez's insults are not limited to the internal opposition. His disparaging remarks against Condoleezza Rice, mentioned earlier, are but a small sample of the litany of abuse that he throws around as a matter of course. In one famous tirade, he called George W. Bush a "donkey," a "child-assassin," a "genocist," a "coward," and a "drunkard."[11] In another notable performance, this one at the United Nations, Chávez referred to Bush as the devil and claimed that the podium where he had stood still reeked of sulfur.[12] Chávez hurled a battery of insults at Spain's former prime minister, José María Aznar, whom he equated with Hitler,[13] at the international meeting of Latin American and European leaders (where Aznar was not present). The tirade ended only when the indignant king of Spain told him to shut up.[14]

Chávez has turned himself into a sewer, spewing whatever vulgarity he can think of at any leader with whom he happens to disagree—and doing so with obvious relish. For example, he refers to the Colombian president, Alvaro Uribe Vélez, as a traitor, a liar, and a coward; the Peruvian president, Alan García, as a thief; the former Mexican president Vicente Fox as George Bush's puppy dog. He says the former British prime minister Tony Blair is immoral and should go to hell; Germany's chancellor, Angela Merkel, should also go to hell; Aznar and Bush are guilty of genocide and possess "less humanity than snakes"; the Peruvian writer Mario Vargas Llosa is a traitor, fascist, and coward; the Peruvian television personality Jaime Bayly is a "fag." Chávez uses the epithet "traitor" rather liberally. Recently he accused the cameramen who work on his television show of being traitors for expecting overtime pay for overtime work. "True revolutionaries," Chávez told them, "are always willing to work for free."[15]

When he expelled the United States ambassador to Venezuela, Patrick Duddy (as a show of "solidarity" with Bolivia's president, Evo Morales, who had expelled the American ambassador to Bolivia a couple of days before), Chávez poured his venom on *all* Americans, saying, "Go to hell, you Yankees of shit, go to hell one hundred times, you Yankees of shit."[16] (He used the phrase *"vayanse al carajo,"* which is hard to translate into English and could be rendered as "go to hell" or as "fuck you.")

Chávez's crudeness is reflected in what he calls his favorite television show in Venezuela, *La Hojilla* ("The Razorblade"), which runs five nights a week on one of the government's television stations. *La Hojilla* is hosted by Mario Silva, a very close ally of Chávez, who appointed him to run for the governorship of Carabobo, one of the country's most important states, in the elections of November 2008. (Silva lost this election.) Silva's show is the only broadcast in the nation competing with Chávez in terms of vulgarity and nastiness. It was on one of his many visits to *La Hojilla* that Chávez said he would "fuck" the opposition candidates "next time they crouch"—a silly but nonetheless crass Venezuelan joke: *"tu te agachas y yo te cojo."* But *La Hojilla* is outrageous on a regular basis, whether or not Chávez is a guest. Even Chavista legislators have called the show offensive: Anyone with whom Silva disagrees—in effect, anyone with whom Chávez disagrees, as Silva is but his mouthpiece—is insulted and humiliated. Opponents are "fags," "assholes," "imbeciles," "Nazis," "assassins," and, above all, "garbage" and "shit." The show's main function is to spread lies and propaganda in favor of Chávez, financed by taxpayers' money. The set is filled with images of Bolívar, Marx, and Lenin. Sitting on Silva's desk are action figures (!) of Chávez, Fidel Castro, and Ernesto "Che" Guevara.

After the conflict between Israel and Lebanon in the summer of 2006, Chávez recalled the Venezuelan ambassador to Israel, accusing Israel of carrying out a genocide in Lebanon "indistinguishable from the Nazi Holocaust." *La Hojilla*, predictably, devoted a series of shows to the problems in the Middle East. On one of these it was suggested that Israel had deliberately gassed 75,000 Lebanese children. In late July 2006, a guest on the program, Santiago Georges, rolled up his sleeves and challenged any Jew watching the show to come to the station for a fistfight. As if to assuage any concern on the part of his co-panelists, Georges stated that there was no reason to worry, since "Jews are a race of snakes; they are cowards—no one will take up the challenge."

The mental health of Venezuelans is threatened not only by Chávez's vulgarity, but also by his asphyxiating presence in the media.

Caracas is now inundated with images of Chávez: the Great Leader playing baseball, the Great Leader in military uniform, the Great Leader kissing a baby, and so on—just as Berlin was wallpapered with Hitler's image, as Baghdad was with Saddam's, as Havana is today with Castro's. This cult of personality is an all-too-familiar aspect of life under a tyrant. It is also well known that Chávez has far surpassed Castro's legendary diatribes; his television shows often last in excess of seven hours. If Venezuelans were politically myopic before Chávez seized power, they have now become deaf as well—or perhaps they are tired of his frequent tirades and simply tune him out.

I suspect that one of Chávez's most repugnant abuses of power is not fully grasped outside Venezuela: the exasperating *cadenas* (i.e., "chains") with which Venezuelans have to deal on a regular basis. These consist of Chávez forcibly "chaining" all the broadcast signals in the country—radio and television—and compelling them to transmit whatever he is saying. If you are watching a sporting event or a movie or the news, or listening to the radio, the signal is suddenly interrupted and you have to watch Chávez do whatever he is doing at the time. With his usual thuggish grin, Chávez taunts the opposition: "You don't like me to be 'chained'—well, what are you going to do about it? Here I am, and I plan to stay for hours upon hours, until I feel like stopping."

On one occasion, Chávez mistakenly thought that his men had chained all the signals, and when he realized that he was not monopolizing every broadcast in the country, he ordered the situation to be rectified immediately. As soon as he was chained, he began to describe the clouds and the breeze in the location from which he was broadcasting—preempting every other program in order to deliver a bizarre impromptu weather report.

While Chávez sometimes chains all broadcasting signals for no reason at all, he chains them more often and for longer periods of time whenever elections are upcoming. Then he floods the airwaves with his own propaganda, increasing the outrageous disparity between his and the opposition's ads.

Freedom of the Press

Chávez's verbal incontinence and his abuse of power are all the more offensive when contrasted with the way in which his repressive laws prevent ordinary people from freely saying what they want, or harass them for doing so. His government passed a law in 2005 called the Law of Social Responsibility in Radio and Television, which fastidiously delimits what radio and television stations are allowed to broadcast.[17] Between 7:00 A.M. and 7:00 P.M., it is forbidden to broadcast anything—even in the news segment—that is not fit to be viewed by children. Between 5:00 A.M. and 11:00 P.M., it is permissible only to broadcast material that children can watch under the supervision of their parents. Thus, it is only for six hours a day, in the wee hours of the night, that television stations are somewhat free to broadcast whatever they want. "Somewhat" free is accurate, for certain things, such as "nakedness without educational purpose" or "subliminal messages," are always forbidden.

The sorts of things prohibited include not only sex and violence, but also abusive language (e.g., swearing)—notwithstanding that Chávez and friends utter obscenities at any hour of the day. There have been countless incidents in which Chávez swears on national television. But things are different for those not on Chávez's side. I will examine a couple of notorious cases.

Chávez's government harshly fined a famous Venezuelan humorist, Laureano Márquez, for writing a rather innocuous column in one of the very few remaining independent newspapers in the country. The fine was roughly US $50,000.[18] In a country where the vast majority of the population makes less than US $250 a month, such a fine is pretty substantial. (The minimum wage in Venezuela is roughly US $200 a month, but a huge percentage of the population—the unemployed, or those in the "informal economy" such as street vendors—make even less.) The fine was paid, but only after public fundraising efforts netted the necessary sum.

Márquez's column appeared in *Tal Cual,* a Venezuelan newspaper edited by Teodoro Petkoff, a former guerrilla leader, left-leaning politician, and strong Chávez critic, on December 15, 2006. It consisted of a fictitious letter written by Rosinés, Chávez's youngest daughter, to the Baby Jesus. (In Venezuela, a Catholic country, children write to the Baby Jesus every Christmas asking him for this or that gift in return for their good behavior during the year.) I shall quote Márquez's letter in full:

> Notice that I am writing to you and not to Santa Claus, as evidence of the desire to reform that motivates me to write this letter. This year I will not say whether I behaved well or badly. You had better judge that yourself, since you silently grasp the shape of our hearts and since you know the truth of our most secret intentions.
>
> I have reached a point in my life when I do not feel like asking you for anything.
>
> I do not know if this is the result of the wisdom that comes with age, or of my disenchantment and lack of enthusiasm, but this time I would like to ask you that, rather than bringing things, you take some away—things that we no longer need, or that have become so ordinary that we no longer question their uselessness nor the way in which they are simply a burden in our lives.
>
> For example: the car. In Caracas, specifically, it has become an unbearable burden.
>
> The economic prosperity of recent years has filled our city with cars to such an extent that even Ilan [a pop singer] has stopped singing his song "I go from Petare toward La Pastora" [from the east to the west in Caracas] because no concert could be long enough to allow him to finish the song.
>
> But I don't want to bother you with minutiae.
>
> Let us focus on the essential:
>
> I know that next year will have its difficulties, but as far as I can remember, every year has some difficulties. As in the movie *Brazil*, our complication engenders smaller complications. Give us the serenity to withstand the difficulties. When we are overwhelmed by anxieties, remind us that one day the sun will be a supernova, everything will inexorably end, and the only thing that will remain, as if floating on air, will be the love that we managed to give or to receive.
>
> Only this I ask of you. Since during these days we all try to spend our time surrounded by the affection of our families, remember those who are currently behind bars for their political opinions. I do not want to make you

sad on your birthday, but in some thirty-three years you too will be behind bars for your political opinions. You, too, will be a scapegoat.

Allow this people to regain their freedom, and to be able to spend Christmas in their homes, surrounded by their relatives. Give at least this sign.

Well, pal, thanks for your time. I say goodbye until next year. May we all be able to eat hallaca in peace,* and may the star of tolerance shine on the Venezuelan sky as a symbol of the redemptive hope that Christmas carries with it.

P.S.: Watch out for Herod, who has it in for you, and for Pilate, who sooner or later will wash his hands.

My purpose in presenting the entire text of the letter is not to endorse it or to praise it as a great piece of satire, but to allow readers to judge for themselves the proportionality, or indeed, the very sanity of the punishment to which Chávez, through one of his numerous "Bolivarian" judges, subjected Márquez.

The case of Laureano Márquez is just one example of the many ways in which freedom of expression is trampled in Venezuela today. Chávez often remarks that there are plenty of media outlets in which he is constantly criticized. He fails to mention that these outlets are becoming fewer and fewer, and they are constantly harassed by his government. Chávez's two-pronged strategy against the free press differs from those of past dictatorships. First, rather than close down all media outlets that do not support his views, Chávez has dug into his deep pockets to buy them out. Some have indeed been closed down, but the vast majority of formerly non-Chavista outlets have simply been bought by Chávez and his chums. According to the international organization Reporters Without Borders, "directly or indirectly, President Chávez now controls almost all of the broadcast media."[19] Second, those ever-decreasing outlets that do not agree with Chávez and have not been sold to him or his cronies are harassed and threatened.

---

*Hallaca is a Venezuelan dish similar to a Mexican tamale, prepared at Christmastime.

Many journalists are either in prison or still on trial for trumped-up charges.[20] Understandably, many journalists have fled the country. It is true that some critics of Chávez's regime still remain in Venezuela, but their numbers are rapidly dwindling as a result of his systematic attacks. At any rate, Chávez's stranglehold on the media renders opposition journalists almost irrelevant, for their share of the market is negligible.

On May 27, 2007, Chávez closed down Venezuela's oldest television station, Radio Caracas Televisión, best known as RCTV. While this measure did provoke some international criticism, many still fail to see the magnitude of what Chávez has done. RCTV was the *only* open-signal Venezuelan television station with national reach, and this is a crucial fact in a country where cable television is an anomaly.

Chávez and his fans have defended the closing of RCTV with two main arguments, both of which are weak at best. First, they have played the euphemism game: RCTV was not "closed"; rather, "its concession was not renewed." True, the government had the right not to renew the concession, but it hardly needs stating that what is permitted and what is desirable or laudable are not the same thing. And however one wishes to describe what happened, the fact is that RCTV no longer broadcasts its open signal and no longer reaches millions of Venezuelan homes.

The second argument made in defense of Chávez's actions is that RCTV was not prohibited from broadcasting *tout court*, but only via open signal; RCTV was free to broadcast via cable or satellite. But this is grossly misleading, first and foremost because cable and satellite television reach a minuscule proportion of the Venezuelan population. The argument is dishonest, too, in that RCTV has had to fight all sorts of legal battles in order to fend off the various attempts by Chávez's regime to prevent it even from broadcasting via cable or satellite. (The case is still open.) Chávez's government also confiscated RCTV's equipment, a move that was not only wrong politically and morally, but also patently illegal. While Chávez had the legal right to close down RCTV, he did not have the right—legal or otherwise—to confiscate RCTV's equipment.

The reasons presented by Chávez for closing RCTV are interesting. He alleges that the station was involved in the coup attempt against him on April 11, 2002. The problems with this position are manifold and rather obvious; but I will focus on just two. First, the Venezuelan Supreme Court (the Supreme Tribunal of Justice), packed with Chávez supporters, declared that there had been no coup in Venezuela, but only a power vacuum after Chávez's secretary of defense, General Lucas Rincón, announced on national television that Chávez had resigned. Second, if there had been a coup, and if individuals associated with RCTV had been involved in it, they should have been brought to trial. I wish to discuss these two problems within the context of the typical pro-Chávez stance, to bring out how untenable the position of Chávez's supporters really is.

Was there a coup? I could be accused of the same thing that I accuse Chávez and his supporters of doing: playing semantic games. While they quibble about "end of concession" as opposed to "closing down," I quibble about "power vacuum" as opposed to "coup d'état." But the cases are different. The fact is that RCTV is no more, whereas the facts about what really happened in Venezuela during those forty-eight hours in which Chávez was out of power remain to be determined.

The "coup leaders"—i.e., the members of the Venezuelan Armed Forces, some of whom were close personal friends of Chávez—repeatedly stated on national television, as the events of April 11 were unfolding, that they were not carrying out a coup d'état. They insisted that they were simply following the Bolivarian Constitution, which obligated them to disobey orders that violated it. Efraín Vásquez Velasco, one of the main leaders of the day's events, admitted on national television, as the events were unfolding, that he was asking for Chávez's resignation with great sorrow, given how much he loved him. He insisted that this was not a coup d'état, and that his actions were mandated by the constitution.

Things were happening at dizzying speed, and no one knew much of anything during that day. Late that night, on national television, General Rincón told the nation that in response to Chávez's activation of

"Plan Avila," which involved shooting at innocent and unarmed civilians, a group of generals had asked Chávez to resign. The so-called coup plotters never fired a gun. According to Rincón, Chávez accepted the request of his generals and tendered his resignation. The next day, Pedro Carmona, who until that day had been the president of the Venezuelan Chamber of Commerce, was sworn in as interim president of Venezuela. He appointed an interim cabinet and, with one single decree, he quickly dissolved the National Assembly and the Supreme Court, nullified the posts of governors and mayors, and changed the name of the country back to the Republic of Venezuela (instead of the Bolivarian Republic of Venezuela).

At this point, the very same generals who had asked for Chávez's resignation, and many of Chávez's most vehement critics (like Teodoro Petkoff), swore not to support Carmona, claiming that *they* had been upholding the law all along. Mere hours after Carmona's infamous decree, Chávez was back inside the Presidential Palace. That is, the main supporters of the "coup" immediately took back their support once they thought that things were not being done in accordance with Venezuelan law; this happened not when Chávez was detained, but when Carmona swore himself in as president. During his absence, Chávez had been at the Venezuelan military base on the island of La Orchila, were he was accompanied by ecclesiastical authorities and was not harmed in any way—a rather strange procedure for a coup.

Months later, Chávez's Supreme Court acquitted all the generals who participated in the events of April 11, 2002, and specifically claimed that there had been no coup d'état, but merely a power vacuum. Chávez's immediate reaction to the court's ruling was to call it a "clump of shit" and say that the only thing the justices who voted this way knew how to do was defecate.[21] Months after this, he went after those justices who had voted for acquittal, and eventually shook up the whole Supreme Court yet again in order to get an even firmer grip on it.

If what happened on April 11 was indeed a coup d'état, it was strikingly *sui generis*. The plotters were close friends of the president. They brandished not weapons but the Venezuelan Constitution, and they even apologized, more or less, for having to go to such lengths. Hours after the alleged resignation of the ousted president, the plotters brought down his successor for disregarding the rule of law. And the plotters were all acquitted by a Supreme Court stacked with supporters of the coup's "victim." Many of these "plotters" still live in Venezuela.

Despite the confusing nature of what happened, Chávez's fans abroad (following his lead) have turned the events into an epic victory for socialism against the evil empire. Consider Kim Bartley's and Donnacha O'Brian's "riveting documentary,"[22] *The Revolution Will Not Be Televised* (AKA *Chávez: Inside the Coup*), which was shown at independent movie theaters in the United States and Europe, to the acclaim of many a naïve and misinformed viewer.

This "documentary" tells a one-sided tale, entirely favorable to Chávez, and fails to mention crucial events that took place during those two days. For example, the declaration of General Lucas Rincón in which he stated that Chávez had resigned is completely omitted. How can a documentary about the coup of April 11, 2002, leave out such a central element? I trust that my readers can come up with an answer on their own.

While the Federation of Venezuelan Movie Directors vehemently objected to the "farce" that *The Revolution Will Not Be Televised* truly is,[23] this objection did not prevent famous movie critics in the United States from lauding it. Roger Ebert, for example, exalted it as a "remarkable documentary" even though he admitted that it is "clearly biased in favor of Chávez." Ebert even ventured into a bit of politics on his own, explaining that the incident can easily and fully be understood if we realize that "it all comes down to oil."[24] Ebert finished his review on an odd note: "Although it is outrageously unfair and indefensible of me, I cannot prevent myself from observing that Chávez and his cabinet have open, friendly faces, quick to smile, and that the faces of his opponents are closed, shifty, hardened."[25] True, this *is* indefensible. More indefensible, however, is the irresponsibility with which Ebert feeds false information to his readers. He claims that Carmona fled to Miami, when in fact he was imprisoned in Venezuela, where he stood trial until he asked for asylum in the Colombian embassy. And Ebert, also glibly and irresponsibly, praises Chávez as having found "fair and obvious" solutions to Venezuela's problems. He would be well served by taking a look at some of the statistics from international organizations that I presented in the previous chapter before he credits Chávez with having solved anything.

The Federation of Venezuelan Movie Directors commissioned Wolfgang Schalk and Thaelman Urguelles to produce a response to the propaganda piece by Bartley and O'Brian. Their film is called *Radiografía de una Mentira* ("X-ray of a Lie"), and it is freely available online.[26] While this documentary does expose the mendacity and tendentiousness of *The Revolution Will Not Be Televised*, and does accurately document the many falsehoods and the questionable tactics of its directors, it is not well known at all. It has not been praised, let alone reviewed, in the *New York Times*, or by Roger Ebert, or by pretty much anyone who praised the "riveting" and "remarkable" documentary to which it is a response.

Let us turn now to the second problem with the attempt to defend Chávez's closing of RCTV on the grounds that the station was involved in the April 11 "coup." While it is by no means clear that a coup had taken place, I will stipulate for the sake of argument that there was a coup. Whether RCTV was a participant in the events is not clear at all. But many of Chávez's supporters, including Rod Stoneman, the executive producer of *The Revolution Will Not Be Televised*, as well as academics and authors from prestigious universities in the United Kingdom, see things differently. Here is the letter of support for Chávez's action that they published in the *Guardian* on May 26, 2007:[27]

> We believe that the decision of the Venezuelan government not to renew the broadcasting licence of RCTV when it expires on May 27 ("Chávez silences critical TV station," May 23; Comment and Letters, May 25) is legitimate given that RCTV has used its access to the public airwaves to repeatedly call

for the overthrow of the democratically elected government of President Hugo Chávez. RCTV gave vital practical support to the overthrow of Venezuela's elected government in April 2002 in which at least thirteen people were killed. In the forty-seven hours that the coup plotters held power, they overturned much of Venezuela's democratic constitution—closing down the elected national assembly, the supreme court and other state institutions.

RCTV exhorted the public to take to the streets and overthrow the government and also colluded with the coup by deliberately misrepresenting what was taking place, and then conducting a news blackout. Its production manager, Andrés Izarra, who opposed the coup, immediately resigned so as not to become an accomplice.

This is not a case of censorship. In Venezuela more than 90 percent of the media is privately owned and virulently opposed to the Chávez government. RCTV, far from being silenced, is being allowed to continue broadcasting by satellite and cable. In Venezuela, as in Britain, TV stations must adhere to laws and regulations governing what they can broadcast. Imagine the consequences if the BBC or ITV were found to be part of a coup against the government. Venezuela deserves the same consideration.

Colin Burgon MP
Dr Julia Buxton
Jon Cruddas MP
Tony Benn
Billy Hayes, General Secretary, CWU
John Pilger
Professor Jonathan Rosenhead LSE
Hugh O'Shaughnessy
Rod Stoneman, Executive Producer, The Revolution Will Not Be Televised
And 16 others

What the signatories do not say is that there is not one iota of evidence linking RCTV, or any of its directors or owners, to any coup whatsoever. In civilized countries, when someone believes that someone else has committed a crime, the only legitimate procedure is for the judicial authorities to determine if in fact a crime has been committed. Neither RCTV nor any of its directors or owners was brought to trial for participation in the events of April 11, 2002.

It would have been easy for Chávez to obtain a (sham) conviction of people associated with RCTV, like the one he secured against Laureano Márquez, given how firm his grip now is on the whole judicial branch. But he did not even bother to take that step. All we have against RCTV is that Chávez says that it was involved in the coup (and remember, we are hypothesizing a coup, even though the Venezuelan Supreme Court expressly denied it). And yet, Chávez's word is enough for the signatories of this letter. They don't need courts of law when they have the solemn word of the Great Leader.

Moreover, and this is also very important, whatever RCTV did or did not do during the events of April 11, 2002 (or in the months before), it did not differ in any significant way from what Venevisión and Televén, the other two open signal television stations in Venezuela, had done. Televén, a much newer and less important broadcaster, has now been bought by Chávez's friends, and so there is no point in closing it. Venevisión, RCTV's traditional rival, is a more interesting story. It is owned by Gustavo Cisneros, one of Venezuela's richest men, and one of the richest men in the world (currently ranked 114th in *Forbes'* list of the richest people, with a net worth of five billion dollars).[28] Cisneros has been on and-off friends with Chávez. When Chávez ran for president in 1998, Cisneros supported him openly. Subsequently they have had a falling-out of sorts. In fact, shortly after April 11, Chávez suggested that Cisneros was an integral part of the "coup." (Chávez used to call Cisneros the "Kapo" of the opposition.) The hostility between the two became so great that in June of 2004—about two months before the referendum seeking to revoke his mandate—Chávez ordered the police to raid Cisneros's properties. Allegedly, these raids revealed all sorts of weapons, which Chávez insisted were to be used in ousting him.[29] Cisneros, for his part, accused the government of harassment.[30]

But a week after the raid on his property, Cisneros was meeting with Chávez and Jimmy Carter, who brokered this mysterious conclave. Whatever happened in the meeting is unknown to the general public; what is clear is that it changed things dramatically. Chávez and Cisneros were friends again. Venevisión stopped criticizing the regime, and Chávez stopped harassing Cisneros. But Chávez surely kept harassing Cisneros's competition, above all RCTV. The fact is that while Venevisión did nothing differently from RCTV during the "coup," and while its broadcasting license expired the same day as RCTV's, its license was renewed and RCTV's was revoked.[31]

If we assume, disregarding all the facts, that there was a coup against Chávez on April 11, 2002, and that RCTV alone was involved in it, the question of the legitimate response from the regime remains unanswered. If all these stipulations are made, then it would follow that some of the owners, shareholders, directors, anchors, etc. of RCTV committed a crime. Yet no one has been criminally charged. Why not? Again, I leave it to my readers to answer on their own. Instead of a criminal proceeding against a coup plotter, what we witnessed was the closing of Venezuela's oldest and most important television network simply because it was inconvenient to the Great Leader.

American Intellectuals

One of the "leading intellectuals" of the United States, the famous MIT professor Noam Chomsky, commented on the RCTV episode during an interview on September 21, 2007. A team of Venezuelans paid by the Venezuelan government had traveled to Boston to interview Chomsky. One member of the team was Eva Golinger, a major supporter and admirer of Chávez.

Golinger is in frequent communication with Chávez's lobbyists in Washington, such as the Venezuela Information Office, an organization financed by Chávez and registered with the U.S. Department of Justice, in accordance with the Foreign Agents Registration Act of 1938. (For more on Chávez's lobby in the United States, see the appendix below.)[32] Golinger is also the author of a truly incredible book, *The Chávez Code: Cracking U.S. Intervention in Venezuela*.[33] The book is incredible because more than a third of it consists of declassified documents from the United States government, which purportedly reveal an American conspiracy to oust Chávez—but which in fact show nothing of the sort. For example, the book contains copies of requests for information made to the CIA as to what the agency knew about conspiratorial activities in Venezuela preceding the events of April 11, 2002. The CIA would respond with boilerplate letters to the effect of: "The CIA can neither confirm nor deny the existence or nonexistence of records responsive to your request."[34] For Golinger and scores of other Chávez fans, this proves that the United States was trying to oust Chávez, even when some of the documents specifically deny any involvement.

Golinger is a very frequent guest on Chávez's favorite television show, *La Hojilla* ("The Razorblade"), which runs on one of the Venezuelan government's television stations and which, as I pointed out before, is known for its vulgarity and nastiness. It was on *La Hojilla*, too, that an interview with Noam Chomsky first aired in Venezuela.

The interviewer begins by asking Chomsky his opinion of Venezuela's book fair, which, the interview claims, has been spearheaded by Hugo Chávez himself. (Actually, the fair existed long before the Chávez presidency.) In the interviewer's opinion, Chávez is "the first great promoter of reading" in Venezuela. Instead of distancing himself from this piece of propaganda, Chomsky applauds Venezuelans for their reading habits—tacitly praising the Great Promoter. Then he manages to shift the conversation to his favorite theme, denigrating the United States, by suggesting that American children do not read as much as Nicaraguan, Mexican, or Venezuelan children.

It would be interesting to see Chomsky try to reconcile this baseless remark with the fact that Chávez's government has excluded books from the list of goods that can be imported into the country with a preferential exchange rate, in effect turning them into luxury items.[35] It is also hard to square Chomsky's comment with the minuscule number of patents and inventions coming from Venezuela, or with the dismal statistics on education presented in the previous chapter. If Venezuelan, Mexican, and Nicaraguan children read more than American children, it is evidently not helping them achieve anything of note in the arts and humanities, or in the sciences, or, indeed, in politics.

When the interviewer suggests that Venezuela (i.e., Chávez himself) is "giving constitutional rank to popular power," Chomsky again buys the story wholesale, with a gullibility and ignorance unbecoming a university professor. While he admits that there may be problems in the implementation of the mysterious "power to the people" agenda, he is very happy to hear about Chávez's plans because "this is precisely the traditional anarchist ideal," which "the powers of Stalin's Russia, Hitler's Germany, Mussolini's Italy, and Western democracies have cooperated together in crushing."[36] So Western democracies, in Chomsky's opinion, have been in cahoots with the murderous regimes of Stalin, Hitler, and Mussolini. But Chomsky is optimistic that his anarchist ideal, which Western democracies and totalitarian regimes have sought to crush, can be realized in Venezuela—even though Chávez is a power-hungry tyrant who has concentrated more powers in himself than any other Venezuelan leader in history, and who has reversed the efforts of the democratic governments after 1958 to decentralize powers and to create real checks and balances between the branches of government! Chomsky has quite an interesting take on anarchism.

At some point the interviewer asks Chomsky about the closing of RCTV, an event that she describes in laudatory terms. "By closing RCTV," she claims, "Chávez was trying to protect the poor from corporate media." Chomsky's response is rather astonishing:

> Let me say that I agree with the Western criticism in one crucial respect. When they say that nothing like that could happen here, that is correct. But the reason, which is not stated, is that if there had been anything like RCTV in the United States or England or Western Europe, the owners and the managers would have been brought to trial and executed. In the United States executed, in Europe they would have been sent to prison permanently[37] right away, in 2002. I mean, you can't imagine the *New York Times* or CBS News

supporting a military coup which overthrew the government even for a day. The reaction would be to send them to the firing squad. So, yes, [something like the closing of RCTV] would not have happened in the West, because here it never happens this far. But it seems to me that there should have been, that there should be more focus on that.[38]

Chomsky himself has said and written far more critical things—seriously and systematically critical things—about the United States and Western democracies than RCTV ever said or reported about Chávez. I know of no effort on the part of the United States or Western democracies to either execute him or sentence him to life in prison. In fact, Chomsky is regularly afforded police protection when making public appearances.

Had Chomsky lived in Venezuela and criticized Chávez's regime with anything close to the vehemence with which he unloads on the United States on a regular basis, he would be behind bars—as are many of Chávez's Venezuelan critics. Recently Chávez went as far as expelling, in a brutal and repugnant way, José Miguel Vivanco and Daniel Wilkinson, the director and a representative of Human Rights Watch, because their annual report on Venezuela was not to the liking of the Great Leader.[39] Nothing in that report compares remotely to what Chomsky routinely asserts about the United States. His gullibility and superficiality, at least when talking about Venezuela, lend special credence to the accusation that he is the oracle of the "crazy left."

During a forum at the Massachusetts Institute of Technology in early 2006, Chomsky is reported to have "mentioned the Venezuelan process several times as an example to the region and the planet because of its social politics which have had infinite success in education, medical assistance, and in rescuing the dignity of Venezuelans."[40] In an interview on March 18, 2007, Chomsky revealed himself to be rather ignorant about the facts of Venezuelan politics, and he also made a surprising endorsement of a pedestrian cultural relativism. While the interviewers are obviously pro-Chávez, they make an effort to ask something resembling a tough question: "Let's return to some of the criticisms of authoritarianism that have followed term extensions and the recent so-called enabling law." Chomsky replies:

> Well, those laws were passed by the parliament. The parliament happens to be almost completely dominated by Chávez, but the reason for that is that the opposition refuses to take part. Probably under U.S. pressure. I don't like those laws myself. How they turn out depends on popular pressures. They could be steps towards authoritarianism. They could be steps towards implementing constructive programs. It's not for us to say, it's for the Venezuelan people to say, and we know their opinion very well.[41]

Even in such a short passage, Chomsky manages to be wrong in a variety of ways. Most of the "laws" that extend Chávez's term limits are found in the Bolivarian Constitution, which he himself drafted and gave to the "Congresillo." (The Congresillo was an interim all-powerful assembly that stood above all the regular powers of the state—above the Congress, the Supreme Court, and theoretically above Chávez himself.) The opposition tried to participate in that Congresillo, but the electoral formula that Chávez employed prevented them from doing so in any significant way. The opposition has participated in every major election since Chávez won except the last legislative elections, and they refused to participate in those because Chávez's obvious abuse of the system—and of the taxpayers' money—had reached incredible levels. Chomsky's comment that Venezuela's National Assembly is "almost completely dominated by Chávez" is an understatement—it is *entirely* controlled by Chávez's supporters. Needless to say, Chomsky makes no attempt whatsoever to back up his casual assertion that it is "probably under U.S. pressure" that the opposition has stayed on the sidelines, and I know of no evidence whatsoever linking the exasperation of the Venezuelan opposition to United States influence.

Chomsky dares to admit that he himself does not "like those laws." Not that this wimpy criticism of Chávez goes anywhere—for right after this concession, he chalks up the whole issue to a matter of cultural relativism: whether or not he "likes" the laws is irrelevant, so long as the

Venezuelans "like" them. One would like to see Chomsky apply this vulgar relativism to his criticism of the United States or Israel, or other Western democracies!

The enabling laws are mechanisms whereby the Venezuelan legislature authorizes Chávez to issue decrees with the force of laws—in other words, to legislate. They are, it must be acknowledged, not Chávez's invention, for the democratic presidents preceding him also used and abused this insidious practice. But no one ever abused it to the extent that Chávez does.

As I noted above, before Chávez, the enabling laws were narrowly defined, authorizing the president to legislate on one specific matter—usually economic—for a brief period. But Chávez is routinely authorized to legislate all sorts of matters, and for longer periods. The last of these enabling laws expired on July 31, 2008, eighteen months after it had come into play. On the very last day of its validity, Chávez passed laws regulating matters including the structure of the armed forces and of the banking and financial sectors. The opposition was outraged. Luis Miquilena, Chávez's former right-hand man and president of the Congresillo that gave these powers to Chávez in the first place, saw this flurry of last minute laws as "an ambush attempting to introduce via contraband the constitutional reform that the people rejected" in the constitutional referendum of December 7. Miquilena dubbed Chávez's actions "felonious."[42]

The whole discussion of the enabling laws is more than a tad moot, however. After all, Chávez does as he wishes with or without them. The purpose of these laws seems to be maintaining the façade of democracy.

And yet, Chomsky remains silent about how the Venezuelan legislature has effectively committed suicide, as has the Venezuelan Supreme Court, filled as it is with Chávez's friends in what amounts to lifelong appointments. For Chomsky, this state of affairs is fine as long as (some) Venezuelans approve it. He also remains silent about Chávez's anti-Semitism, so thoroughly documented by, for example, the Anti-Defamation League.[43] And this man who speaks so irresponsibly about matters of which he is fundamentally ignorant is an "Institute Professor" at MIT, one of the most prestigious institutions in the United States.

Another case of academic myopia with regard to Venezuela is Brian Leiter, a philosopher of law who has managed to appoint himself the Grand Evaluator in professional philosophy and law. His extremely influential "Philosophical Gourmet Report" makes philosophy department chairs across the United States tremble. Leiter's advisory board includes prominent, serious philosophers, but one cannot help wondering whether his gossip and rumors come from this board as well.[44]

Leiter has discussed the way in which "the right-wing media in the U.S.—and not just the far right, but the 'normal' right (e.g., *The New York Times*)—have characterized recent moves by Venezuelan President Chávez to 'rule by decree' (for eighteen months) as setting the country on the road to authoritarianism." Distancing himself from the "right-wing media," Leiter tells us that "Chávez has, of course, been a pointed (and accurate) critic of Bush and the U.S., and has created in Venezuela an alternative to the neoliberal paradigm favored by the ruling elites in the capitalist pseudo-democracies." Upset with the "smear jobs" that even the "'liberal' media" have perpetrated upon poor Chávez, Leiter urges us to pay attention to a "more benign view."[45] This particular view comes from none other than Gregory Wilpert, one of Chávez's acolytes! I have already given examples of the depth and rigor of Wilpert's book, *Changing Venezuela by Taking Power: The History and Politics of the Chávez Government*. Wilpert, moreover, runs his own website in support of Hugo Chávez and is connected to Venezuela's paid lobbyists in Washington.[46]

Leiter appears to agree with pretty much everything Wilpert has to say about Chávez. He even volunteers a strange analogy with reference to the concern, reported by Wilpert, that some Venezuelans felt about the absence of checks and balances. "These worries were raised in the U.S. when we had one-party control of the executive and legislative branches," Leiter remarks. Then he suggests that "separation of powers really only acts as a check when the branches are controlled by opposition parties—and even then, as the U.S. again illustrates, the limits on executive power may be of limited significance when the 'opposition' party represents just a different wing of the ruling class."[47]

This is a bizarre view of how the American system works, and the comparison to Venezuela is absurd. The Grand Evaluator turned Champion of the Proletariat apparently fails to see that never in American history has one party controlled *all* the seats in Congress, after *all* opposition parties in unison declared their exasperation with the president's abuse of power and refused to participate in sham elections. Never has a United States president been above the law, as Chávez clearly is; never has a United States president openly asserted that those government officials who do not assent to his own omnipotence are traitors. Never has a United States president illegally appointed all justices of the Supreme Court.[48]

These are matters of fact. Leiter is simply wrong, and an embarrassment to his profession, in asserting that the separation of powers is valuable "only" if the branches of government are controlled by different parties. It may be true that if the different branches are controlled by the same party, this *diminishes* the efficacy of the checks and balances. But it takes entirely too much cynicism to suggest, as Leiter does, that if the branches are controlled by the same party, the checks and balances become utterly useless. Many a time, a member of one party has followed his duty as a public servant and curbed the power of a fellow party member in another (or the same) branch. Leiter's cynical view of the separation of powers speaks volumes about his understanding of democracy.

Leiter's acquaintance with the law also seems dubious. He approvingly quotes Wilpert saying that

> the Venezuelan National Assembly may also modify or rescind law-decrees, at any time, should it feel the need to do so. This is quite unlike the enabling law in the U.S., known as the "Fast Track" law, where the president may sign

international treaties that are automatically binding and not open to revision or rescinding by the population.[49]

It is simply false to assert that the "Fast Track" legislation is automatically binding on anyone. Congress always has the right to vote down an agreement struck between the president and a foreign country; what it cannot do is *amend* the agreement.[50] Whether good or bad, "Fast Track" legislation in the United States merely seeks to avoid filibustering; it does not give any new powers to the president. It has been granted to the president in narrow areas and with a comprehensive set of limitations, as would have been clear to Wilpert and Leiter had they simply read the relevant legislation.

Wilpert remarks that the Venezuelan National Assembly can modify or rescind any law at any time. Well, this is no less the case in the United States, or in any civilized country—the essential function of the legislative branch is to legislate. As for "the population" being able to revise and rescind, again, Wilpert is not quite right: The population of Venezuela does not have the right to revise laws. It has the right to *vote down* or *disapprove* certain laws. The right becomes effective if 5 percent of the voters request it and, as Article 74 of the Bolivarian Constitution stipulates, if the laws are not about "budget, public finances, amnesty, and those which protect, guarantee, or develop human rights, and [sic] those which approve international treatises." Chávez, via enabling laws, can legislate on any matter he sees fit, including those matters regarding which the people cannot opine.[51]

Through enabling laws, Chávez has created new crimes, in effect violating his own Bolivarian Constitution—a situation that is reminiscent of the infamous *Gesetz zur Behebung der Not von Volk und Reich* (Law to Remedy the Distress of the People and the Nation) in Nazi Germany, which specifically allowed for deviations from the constitution by the executive. And yet, Chávez's enabling law is even more extreme than Hitler's *Ermächtigungsgesetz*. After all, Hitler was enabled merely to legislate on matters limited to budgeting and borrowing, whereas Chávez's enabling laws allow him to legislate in any area whatsoever, including criminal law.

The crucial point which Wilpert fails to mention is that *never* has a law passed by Chávez been modified or voted down by either the National Assembly or the populace; such a possibility has never even been broached. With Chávez controlling all the powers of government, and given the precedent of harassment connected with Chávez's illegal use of the Lista Tascón and other such lists of voters, it seems hard to imagine how such a revision or strike-down could ever succeed, even if it were attempted.

As for Chávez's academic acolytes, Wilpert seems doomed to remain confined to his obscurish website. But Leiter, a few months after he made these posts about Venezuela, was appointed the "John P. Wilson Professor of Law and Director, Center for Law, Philosophy, and Human Values" at the University of Chicago—perhaps even more impressive than his previous title, "Hines H. Baker & Thelma Kelley Baker Chair in Law and Professor of Philosophy" at the University of Texas-Austin. Like Chomsky, he may have credible credentials in his academic field, but he evidently violates Socrates' injunction not to talk about what you do not know. The intellectual irresponsibility that Chomsky and Leiter exhibit when they talk about Venezuela casts doubt on the overall health of their intellectual habits. But at least Chomsky, unlike Leiter, "disliked" Chávez's enabling laws.

The Rest of the American Intelligentsia

If reputed university professors in the United States, like Noam Chomsky and Brian Leiter, are so wrong about what happens in Venezuela and about Venezuela's history, what can we expect from those without doctorates? Predictably, Chávez has many supporters in "progressive" circles in the United States and Europe: the likes of Michael Moore, Cindy Sheehan, and so on. But Chávez has a particularly strong group of fans in Hollywood. Danny Glover (whose movie projects Chávez now bankrolls),[52] Sean Penn, Harry Belafonte, Naomi Campbell ("the supermodel turned Latin American economic specialist," as Tony Allen-Mills wittily put it),[53] Peter Coyote, and Kevin Spacey, among others, all fawn over the Great Leader.

In a blurb for Charles Hardy's *Cowboy in Caracas,* Coyote tells us, "Before we take one more bite of the propaganda sandwich our government offers us to nourish their [sic] view that Hugo Chávez is a monster ... Read this important book, and drop the propaganda sandwich in the trash where it belongs."[54] It is hard to decide what is more grotesque: Coyote's ignorance of Venezuelan politics or his nutritional metaphors. Hardy's book is nothing more than a poorly researched panegyric, as is the book by his fellow Maryknoll missionary, Bart Jones, titled *¡Hugo! The Hugo Chávez Story from Mud Hut to Perpetual Revolution.*[55] Yet another Maryknoll missionary, Roy Bourgeois, had a reaction bordering on a paroxysm after he met with Hugo Chávez.[56] Of all religious groups, except for the militant Muslims of Hezbollah, the Maryknoll Catholic missionaries seem to be the fondest admirers of Hugo Chávez and his revolution.[57]

Human motivation can be so multifarious and inscrutable that it is hard to understand what exactly gathers all these individuals together in supporting a regime about which they know so little, and which has so evidently trampled many a mark of civilization. But it is tempting to suggest that, in addition to a generic fondness for "revolutionaries," the support flows, in the final analysis, from the following concatenation of ideas (for to call this an "argument" is stretching it). Most of those in the hodge-podge club of Chávez fans dislike George W. Bush for a variety of reasons; some of them also dislike Western values, or capitalism, or the United States in general, but the dislike of Bush seems to be the strongest. And thus: Chávez insults Bush; therefore, Chávez must be great. Q.E.D.

For someone like Sean Penn to admit that he became interested in Chávez for this reason is, perhaps, something to be indulged or ignored.[58] But for university professors all over America and Western Europe to do so, implicitly or otherwise, is nothing short of appalling.

Most of the many books available about Chávez are written by express or tacit admirers of Chávez: the likes of Richard Gott, Greg Wilpert, Bart Jones, and Eva Golinger. There are some intellectuals, however, who try to be objective. Somewhere between the rarified air of American academe and the intoxicated air of Hollywood we find the so-called cultural media, like the *New Yorker* and the *New York Review of Books*. Here, too, Chávez has more support than he deserves.

The first of Jon Lee Anderson's sprawling, self-indulgent pieces on Chávez for the *New Yorker,* published on September 10, 2001, is tellingly titled "The Revolutionary: The President of Venezuela Has a Vision, and Washington Has a Headache."[59] Weighing in at almost 13,000 words, the piece is as littered with inaccuracies as the other panegyrics I have discussed. For instance: "Chávez is a mestizo Creole— just as Simón Bolívar was." It should read: "Unlike Simón Bolívar, but like the majority of his other predecessors, Chávez is a mestizo Creole." Stating the matter truthfully, however, makes the ominous overtones of racial tension disappear: Chávez's "race," as I mentioned above, does not differ significantly from the "race" of his predecessors. Similarly, Anderson remarks that Yare, the prison to which Chávez was sent after his attempted coup in 1992, "is an awful place." This is somewhat misleading. If Anderson had acknowledged that *all* prisons in Venezuela are truly awful places, in which rape and murder occur frequently, it would have stripped the statement of its heft and relevance. Revealing that Chávez was housed in a relatively nice part of the prison, where he enjoyed his own personal library and regularly met with visitors— many of whom later became members of his many cabinets—would also have helped put things in perspective.

Anderson's piece contains a great deal of debatable and condescending social commentary: For instance, middle-class Venezuelans "have adopted a distinctly North American approach to living." Anderson's evidence for this notion: "Those who can afford it drive cars, carry cell phones, eat fast food, and shop in malls"—as opposed, perhaps, to riding on donkeys, communicating with smoke signals, eating home-made casseroles, and trading by barter. Would that be the non–North American way? Another example: after skimming through the current bestseller lists in Venezuela and strolling through some shopping malls, Anderson is confident enough to pronounce categorically that "Venezuelans are great believers in miracles." (Are these books on miracles which Anderson finds so abundant the same books that Chomsky applauds Venezuelans for reading?)

Anderson does admit that Chávez had been "conspiring"—against legitimate, democratic governments, I might add—since 1982; and he notes, *en passant,* Chávez's friendship with the "neofascist and holocaust denier" Norberto Ceresole. But these concessions are minor. The essential image of Chávez that emerges from Anderson's piece is that of a "provocative" but charismatic "natural showman" who is a fighter for freedom and justice.

Aside from Anderson's multiple conversations with Chávez himself, his main source, at least regarding the Great Leader's personality, was Edmundo Chirinos, a notorious member of the Venezuelan intelligentsia. While he spends considerable time describing Chirinos's physical appearance—and even that of his office—Anderson neglects to inform us that in the 1980s Chirinos had been the Communist Party's presidential candidate or that, much more importantly, he was a high officer of Hugo Chávez's presidential campaign in 1998. Surely there were other psychiatrists available in Caracas, if what Anderson wanted was an objective view. Incidentally, in July 2008, Chirinos, who like so many other early supporters had become estranged from Chávez, was indicted for the brutal murder of a young woman who had been his patient. Now, at the age of seventy-three, he lives under house arrest, and the evidence against him seems overwhelming. So this was one of Anderson's most important sources, and a man with strong personal ties to Chávez.

In June 2008, almost seven years after his first article on Chávez, Anderson wrote another long piece (ca. 9,000 words) for the *New Yorker* titled "Fidel's Heir: The Influence of Hugo Chávez." Matter-offactly, Anderson notes that "in the past four years, Venezuela has spent four billion dollars on foreign arms purchases, mostly from Russia," and tells how Chávez suggested to him that this buying spree was "to avoid ending up like Saddam." In a similarly laconic vein, Anderson reports that "there is also evidence that Chávez has fostered a relationship with the Colombian Marxist guerrilla organization, Fuerzas Armadas Revolucionarias de Colombia, FARC." He writes about the honors that Chávez bestowed on the "good revolutionary" Raul Reyes, the high-ranking member of FARC who was killed by Colombian government forces in March 2008. In spite of Chávez's legendary butchering of the Spanish language, Anderson tells us that he "has a gospel preacher's deftness with language," along with "an actor's ability to evoke emotions." (Sure, like when he narrates his diarrhea bouts.) There is no discernible reaction from Anderson to the fact that Chávez has asserted that "he would like to stay in power until 2050, when he would be ninety-six years old."

Unfortunately, it is not only Anderson's overly benign take on Chávez and his Bolivarian Revolution that remains intact after seven years of well-documented political and human rights abuses by Chávez's regime. His version of Venezuelan history is blatantly inaccurate and tendentious. For example, he claims that Teodoro Petkoff "ran against Chávez in the 2006 Presidential election." But Anderson is wrong again. Petkoff had been proposed as a viable candidate, and while he conditionally agreed, he also insisted that there should be only one candidate from the whole opposition. When it became obvious that the best candidate was Manuel Rosales, Petkoff ended his preliminary bid. He was never on a ballot against Chávez, and thus he never ran against Chávez.

Anderson asserts that "Chávez was imprisoned, along with his co-conspirators. They were released two years later, in 1994, after Pérez was impeached for corruption, and the criminal charges against them were dismissed." The errors in this passage go beyond the problem of superficial research. Anderson makes it sound as if there were a connection between Pérez's impeachment and Chávez's release. There was none, as you may recall from my discussion of these events above. And the charges against Chávez (and co-conspirators) were not dismissed, either. In an opportunist move, Caldera ordered that Chávez's trial be stopped. There was not even a pardon, since the trial had not concluded; it had not even started in any meaningful sense. To say that charges are dismissed is to imply that the charges lacked merit, and this is not at all what happened.

Given the tendentiousness of Anderson's analysis, it is not surprising that he would perceive Chávez to be the star at the meeting of Latin American heads of state held in the Dominican Republic in May 2008, a meeting where tensions in the region were dramatically lowered. Tensions had been running high after Venezuela unilaterally mobilized its army to the border with Colombia, in response to Colombia's "aggression" against Ecuador at the beginning of March. What was Colombia's aggression? It bombed a FARC base a couple of miles inside Ecuadorian territory. (I will return to this incident later.) In Anderson's view, "Uribe understood that he had been temporarily outmaneuvered" by Chávez, even though, by any sensible account of what happened, Uribe was a clear winner in the session. Uribe, after all, left the meeting unscathed; he had not been reprimanded in any concrete way for his violation of Ecuadorian sovereignty. Chávez, however, looked more buffoonish than usual, and after he had ridiculously—and dangerously—mobilized his troops on the Colombian border, he ended up embracing Uribe and wasting yet more Venezuelan taxpayers' money on demobilizing the troops a week later. While this demobilization lessened the danger in the situation, it did not diminish Chávez's stupidity. A couple of months after Anderson's article in the *New Yorker*, Chávez and Uribe had become great friends again. Chávez has claimed that what happened between them in the past is just like what happens between husband and wife. (He used the same marital analogy to explain his sudden reconciliation with the king of Spain in July 2008.)

In her articles on Chávez for the *New York Review of Books* in October 2008, Alma Guillermoprieto tries to bring some much-needed balance to describing the highly polarizing Venezuelan situation, attempting to avoid the extremes of "bilious anger or unconditional devotion."[60] If only, Guillermoprieto describes Chávez's insatiable and dangerous narcissism and his conspiracies against democratically elected governments as being at times "endearing." In the name of "balance," she somehow renders Chávez's power-hungry machinations as "idealistic, vague, and romantic." And yet, alongside the many authors who are infatuated with Chávez, Guillermoprieto comes across as somewhat successful in even-handedness, though this success comes by way of a familiar superficiality of tone. We find the usual pro-Chávez pieties: He was born into a "dirt-poor family"; the Venezuelan opposition is motivated by racism; and so on. There is no mention of the fact that Chávez's socioeconomic and ethnic background is indistinguishable from that of the vast majority of the presidents in the allegedly oligarchic *ancien régime*.

Guillermoprieto's superficiality begins with the fact that she does not reference a single Venezuelan historian, in spite of Venezuela's tradition of excellence in this field. Instead, she turns to Richard Gott, who has no formal training in Venezuelan history and is an open Chávez supporter—thus neither a qualified nor an objective source. (The same ideological proximity to Chávez is found in another of Guillermoprieto's sources: Ernesto "Che" Guevara's daughter Aleida.) Guillermoprieto uncritically accepts Gott's account—which in effect is Chávez's account—of Venezuela's "five republics," although, as we saw in the first chapter, it is highly contested by Venezuelan historians. Two of the four books that she reviews are "in-house," partisan jobs, while only one of them is written by someone formally trained in political theory—though Guillermoprieto refers to the author, Colette Capriles, who was trained by the late Luis Castro Leiva, arguably the finest Venezuelan political philosopher of the twentieth century, as a mere "columnist."

All that Guillermoprieto tells us about Capriles's book is that it is "convoluted" but "sometimes brilliant," and that Capriles writes as though mildly depressed.[61]

Guillermoprieto claims that Chávez has "two political parties." Depending on how you count, however, the number of "Chávez's parties" ranged, at the time she wrote, from zero to more than fifteen. Guillermoprieto's individuating principles remain a mystery. She refers to Isaías Rodríguez, who at the time was Chávez's *fiscal general* (and formerly vice president—appointed to both posts in violation of laws that Chávez himself had championed), as a "member of cabinet," something which, in accordance with Venezuelan law, he most emphatically was not. This is an important point insofar as the crucial functions of the *fiscal general* (broadly similar to those of attorney general in the United States) are to protect the people from governmental abuses. Thus, unlike a cabinet member, the *fiscal general* is not supposed to be partial, much less openly loyal, to the president, as Rodríguez has always been.

Moreover, Guillermoprieto refers to Acción Democrática (AD), the most important political party in Venezuelan history, and indeed one of the most important in all Latin America, as "Alianza Democrática." While Guillermoprieto's remarks about how this party degenerated into a terribly corrupt and illegitimate organization are essentially correct, she nonetheless is silent about the fact that this truly popular party laid the foundations for democracy in Venezuela through, for example, the establishment of universal, secret, and uncoerced suffrage. Similarly, she says precious little about the ways in which the degeneration of Acción Democrática led to an impasse between party leaders and Carlos Andrés Pérez, one of its most prominent members, while the latter was president in the early 1990s. This impasse, largely the result of Pérez's decision to appoint the most qualified Venezuelans rather than his party cronies to key cabinet positions, ultimately weakened his power.

The Perils of Chávez

I will be satisfied if the preceding pages have contributed to the sorely needed effort of presenting Venezuelan history in an unbiased way, and in a way that helps explain Chávez's arrival and continuation in power. I hope to have shown that Chávez is a buffoon, that his revolution is a failure, and that some commentators in the United States—both in academia and in leading cultural magazines—are fundamentally wrong in their assessments of him. But what about the threat he poses? Aside from his vulgarity and insults, and the harm he may have caused the Venezuelan people, is he really a dangerous man?

In broad outline, I have answered this question already. Someone with his psychological characteristics who happens to possess nearly infinite financial resources (above all from oil revenues, though he constantly increases taxes on Venezuelans), who hates the United States and the West generally, and who is buying weapons at an alarming rate is obviously a danger. But I wish now to discuss the dangers that Chávez represents in more specific ways.

Let us begin by considering Chávez's friends. The only thing more impressive than the list of people he has insulted is the list of people of whom he speaks glowingly. The ranks of Chávez's heroes include many champions of freedom, democracy, and peace: Fidel Castro; Ernesto "Che" Guevara; Carlos the Jackal (Ilich Ramírez Sánchez); the Iranian president, Mahmoud Ahmadinejad, whom he calls his "brother" and "partner"; Hassan Nasrallah, the leader of Hezbollah; Vladimir Putin and Dmitry Medvedev, with whom he has formed a "triumvirate of brothers and partners"; Alexander Lukashenko, the president of Belarus, another "partner"; Saddam Hussein, his "brother" and "brave soldier of freedom"; Robert Mugabe, another "brother," also a homophobe and longtime dictator, to whom Chávez pledged support in the midst of "international efforts" to oust him;[62] the rebels of the Colombian terrorist group FARC, and as many other terrorist groups around the globe as he can find.

But it is not the list alone that is impressive. These relationships all seem to be affected by a certain madness. If the word "madness" sounds extreme, a letter that Chávez wrote to Carlos the Jackal may illustrate the point:

> Miraflores, March 3, 1999
> Citizen
> Ilich Ramírez Sánchez
> Present
> Distinguished Compatriot:
>
> Swimming in the depths of your solidarity-filled letter, I was able to discern the sounds of the thoughts and the feelings, because everything has its time: there is a time to gather stones, and a time to cast them aside ... a time to give warmth to the revolution and a time to ignore it; a time to advance dialectically, uniting whatever should be united amongst the pugnacious classes, and a time to facilitate the confrontation between said classes, according to the thesis of Ivan Ilich Ulianov. There is a time to fight for ideals, and a time in which we cannot but value the struggle itself.... A time of opportunity, a time for the refined sense of smell, and for the menacing instinct to reach the propitious psychological moment in which Ariadne, invested in laws, would weave the thread that would allow us to leave the labyrinth....
>
> The Liberator Simon Bolívar, whose theories and praxis inform the doctrine that underlies our revolution, in a sphinx-like invocation to God allowed this phrase to drop, premonitory of his own physical disappearance: How will I ever be able to leave this labyrinth...! The phrase, of a tacit meaning and collected by his family doctor, the Frenchman Alejandro Próspero Réverend in his memoirs, is a profound and illuminating flame on the road that we follow.
>
> Another Frenchman, Alexandre Dumas, ends his work *The Count of Montecristo* with this phrase from Jesus: "The life of men is based on two verbs: to trust and to wait," inducing us to think that at the end of the battle some Supreme Someone will appear and with supreme wisdom, like Abbot Faria inspired the way out, wrapped in new revolutionary syntheses in approximation to the God that each one carries in his heart.
>
> Let us with Bolívar say that time will do miracles only insofar as we maintain a righteous will and insofar as we abide by those necessary relations that derive from the essence of things. Humanity is only one and there is no

space-time magnitude that could stop the thought of the Caracas hero. Let us with him say:

"I feel that my soul's energy rises up, and broadens and equals always the magnitude of the dangers. My doctor has told me that my soul needs to be fed with dangers in order for me to remain sane, in such a way that as He created me, God allowed this tempestuous revolution, so I could live occupied with my special destiny."

With profound faith in the cause and in the mission, for now and forever!

Hugo Chávez Frías[63]

As if there were not enough substantive similarities between Chávez and Hitler, their literary style is also very similar. Chávez's prose and imagery in this letter are eerily reminiscent of Hitler's *Mein Kampf*. I have endeavored to bring some intelligibility to the letter, and I can assure readers that my translation is much more intelligible than the text in the original Spanish.

As for the substance of the letter, it is no better than the style. Who is Ivan Ilich Ulianov? Is Chávez confusing Tolstoy's Ivan Ilyich Golovin with *Vladimir* Ilyich Ulianov (Lenin)? It would not be surprising. And what, at any rate, does this character have to do with a Greek goddess of fertility? Or with Dumas's famous tale of revenge? Or with the notes that Bolívar's doctor took at his deathbed? Nothing at all, of course. And yet, despite this sort of incoherent babble, people ranging from Sean Penn to Noam Chomsky praise Chávez's way with words and the depth of his ideas.

Perhaps the only things clear from this letter are that Chávez respects and sympathizes with Carlos the Jackal and thinks they are both embarked on the same project.[64] The Jackal's relatives, for example, understood the letter to mean that Chávez "would do anything in his power to protect the Jackal's rights."[65] This is not something to sneeze at, given the Jackal's criminal record. I cannot help but enjoy imagining the Jackal's reaction to this cryptic, crazy letter.

Chávez's devotion to Fidel Castro is even more fervent. During a recent speech, Chávez recited his own version of Christianity's most famous prayer, the Lord's Prayer, substituting Fidel's name for God's—and adding a bit of the unmistakably Chavista scatological touch. In a state of rapture, Chávez said:

> Our Father, who art in the Earth, in the Water and in the Air, Fidel;
> Here you are multiplied, Father, in us, your sons and your daughters;
> This is why I say: long live Fidel, shit![66]

But Chávez's insanity is not just a matter of flowery rhetoric and corny clichés, sprinkled with vulgarity. For example, on March 1, 2008, the Colombian armed forces conducted an operation that killed Raul Reyes, an important member of Colombia's infamous FARC, officially considered a terrorist group by both the United States and the European Union.[67] As noted above, this operation extended about one or two miles inside Ecuadorian territory, where FARC had set up some sort of permanent camp. A diplomatic conflict ensued, as Ecuador complained about the violation of its sovereignty—without mentioning that it had allowed (or failed to prevent) FARC to have a permanent military base inside its own borders, presumably a much more serious "violation of sovereignty." Missing the limelight, Chávez called President Uribe a liar, a criminal, a traitor, and a servant of the evil empire (the United States), among other epithets, on national television.[68] And during his weekly television program, *Aló Presidente,* he issued an order to his bewildered secretary of defense: "Mobilize ten battalions of the Venezuelan army to the border with Colombia."[69]

Mobilizing troops on such a large scale, on a whim, as Chávez did, speaks volumes about his trigger-happy temperament—the same sort of temperament which, according to his former friends who briefly ousted him in 2002, he manifested against the innocent, unarmed Venezuelan population, and which was the cause of his brief removal from office. But Chávez's deferential, protective attitude toward FARC also says a great deal about where his allegiances lie.

The Colombian army seized personal computers belonging to the FARC leader Raul Reyes from the compound where he was killed. These computers allegedly revealed all manner of connections between Chávez and FARC. Moreover, they revealed that considerable material support was going from Chávez to FARC, in both money and weapons. Of course, Chávez denies this, and I have no way of ascertaining the veracity of this report. But there are reasons to trust the findings. First, Interpol, the largest international police organization, whose constitution forbids it from engaging in any political activity, performed an analysis of the computer and concluded that there had been no tampering whatsoever with its contents.[70] Second, Chávez's own behavior amply attests to his support of FARC.

When the Colombian government dismantled FARC's camp in late February 2008, killing Reyes in the process, Chávez accused the regime of being mad and murderous. He dubbed the elimination of Reyes a "cowardly assassination."[71] He repeatedly referred to Reyes as a "revolutionary commander," in fact a "good revolutionary," to the applause of his captive *Aló Presidente* audience. Chávez further argued that he could be trusted on this point, since he knew Reyes "in person." On national television, Chávez paid homage to his "fallen comrade" with a minute of silence.[72]

While most Western nations classify FARC as a terrorist organization, Chávez defends and even praises it as an "insurgent force." Addressing the Venezuelan National Assembly, Chávez unabashedly stated:

> I say it even though someone may get annoyed. FARC and ELN are not terrorist organizations of any sort; they are armies, true armies, which occupy a space. Recognition must be given to FARC and ELN; they are insurgent forces, which have a political project, which have a Bolivarian project—a project that we, over here, respect.[73]

FARC leaders have always been very nicely treated by Chávez, although the honeymoon is sometimes interrupted by Chávez's inconsistent and empty declarations condemning terrorism. Even these declarations are accompanied by indictments against the United States, which Chávez constantly tells us is the "greatest terrorist in the world."

Chávez has in effect given sanctuary to FARC terrorists inside Venezuela. He warned Uribe not to attempt in Venezuela what he did in Ecuador (attacking and dismantling a FARC base), as it would be an act of war. Bumbling his way through language, he initially used the Latin expression *casus belli*, though he butchered it by saying "causus bellis."[74] Eventually he managed to convey his threat in Spanish, claiming that Colombia had put all of South America on the brink of war. But the Colombian military never mobilized its troops, not even in response to Chávez's own menacing mobilization. The only person who put the continent on the brink of war was Chávez.

Furthermore, Chávez claimed that the "murderous action" against FARC had not really been planned by the Colombian government, which in his view was but a puppet of the American Empire.[75] Similarly, after Russian troops invaded Georgia a few months later, Chávez's government issued an official press release in which it stated that "the military offensive carried out by Georgia in South Ossetia, without any valid justification, ignited the flames of war in the Caucasian region," and added, "this conflict was planned, prepared and ordered by the government of the United States."[76]

It is, I hope, unnecessary to dwell on the absurdity of Chávez's version of events in Georgia in August 2008. Predictably, he sided with those most clearly opposed to the United States. But it is not merely that Chávez favors anyone he thinks dislikes the United States, and the West; he actually blames the United States government for anything negative that happens in the world. That goes not only for human acts, but also for acts of nature: Chávez has repeatedly blamed George W. Bush's government for tsunamis in the Indian Ocean, for hurricanes in the Caribbean, and for the 1999 mudslides in Venezuela.[77]

Chávez's rapport with FARC led Colombia's opportunistic president, Alvaro Uribe, to seek his services as an intermediary with the terrorist group, trying to procure freedom for some of the hundreds of innocents whom FARC had kidnapped, and whom it was using as bargaining chips. Some of these hostages had been in captivity for more than six years. But what Uribe saw as an opportunity to liberate the hostages, Chávez saw as an opportunity to advance his agenda of presenting himself as a great humanitarian. Accordingly, Chávez publicized his own role and greatly exaggerated his imminent accomplishments. Venezuelan television crews were sent to the jungle, where members of Chávez's cabinet wore camouflage suits and spoke via radio with both Chávez and the terrorists. Even the famed American movie director Oliver Stone came down to film the epic liberation of the hostages. (Stone offered the same sort of childish support to Chávez that the likes of Danny Glover and Sean Penn usually afford him, and is now scheduled to release a documentary on Chávez's life.)[78]

Chávez's mission was, as usual, a failure. One of the hostages to be liberated, a child, turned out not to have been in FARC's hands to begin with; he had been placed in an orphanage years earlier. The episode would have been a humiliating fiasco, as the press initially called it,[79] had FARC not released a handful of hostages some weeks later. But even this late release, whose connection to Chávez is unclear, was not what Chávez had advertised. The fact is that Chávez proved to be so useless that mere weeks after Uribe had agreed to his brokering services, he asked Chávez to stop "helping" him.

The highest-visibility hostage in FARC's hands was a former Colombian presidential candidate, Ingrid Betancourt, who had been held captive for many years and had been seen in recent footage looking frail and emaciated. A few weeks after killing Reyes, and with FARC evidently weakened, Uribe, in a daring mission, fooled the disconcerted FARC and rescued Betancourt, along with three American citizens and a few other hostages—without firing a single shot. Upon her liberation, Betancourt, who is politically opposed to Uribe, said that she had thought the guerrillas' camouflage was Venezuelan (but she was not sure—the uniforms could have been Brazilian). As to the fact that the FARC terrorists "adore" Chávez and that "for the guerrilla, Chávez is a hero," she had no doubts.[80]

While Chávez simply could not admit it, Uribe's success, without his help, was a blow to his ego and to his international image. In fact, he and his spokesmen have sought every way to discredit Uribe's success. Perhaps the most outlandish of these Chavista efforts was the thesis put forth by Chávez's deputies that Uribe had not really captured Betancourt, but that FARC, in a spontaneous and noble "act of humanism," had given her up.[81] We are thus to assume that FARC's "humanism" went so far as giving up some of its own members—those who were captured during the operation.

The ease with which Chávez, in a calculated public relations move, claimed that Uribe was now his "brother" (perhaps a demotion from the rank of "husband" that Chávez had conferred upon him previously?), and treated him with great warmth, should not lead us to ignore the equal ease with which he put Venezuela on the brink of war against Colombia a few weeks earlier. His sympathies are with the terrorist group, not with Colombia's democratically elected president. And his malapropisms and inconsistencies should not obscure the fact that Chávez, as he himself incessantly repeats, is sympathetic to any organization that is against the United States—or the West.

Among the loudest anti-American and anti-Western voices nowadays, we of course find Iran, as well as many groups associated with Islamic fundamentalism. Predictably, Chávez has strengthened relationships with Iran and with terrorist groups like Hamas and Hezbollah. For example, and in spite of the great distance between Venezuela and Iran, on March 2, 2007, Chávez inaugurated a weekly long-haul flight from Caracas to Damascus and to Tehran. His secretary of infrastructure claimed that this flight "goes far beyond the commercial: It is the union of three regions which will facilitate cultural exchange." The launch of the Airbus 340 flight, he said, was a "historic moment."[82] The press release from the state-owned Venezuelan airline Conviasa ends: "With the incorporation of this airplane, Conviasa ratifies the commitment of the National Government and of the Ministry of People's Power for Infrastructure with our brothers in America and the Middle

East."[83] Venezuela's secretary of foreign affairs, Nicolás Maduro, speaking "from his soul," declared that "the two nations are like brothers ... carrying the flags of dignity and sovereignty."[84] Ahmadinejad, for his part, has said that in spite of the geographic distance between the two countries, their "hearts and thoughts are very close."[85] Indeed.

But this long-haul flight is but the tip of the iceberg, for Venezuela and Iran are now partners in many ventures. Swimming in petrodollars, Ahmadinejad and Chávez want to create a fund that will bring "death to U.S. imperialism" and will assist governments that "are making efforts to liberate themselves from the (U.S.) imperialist yoke."[86] Tehran and Caracas also have projects to build tractors, trucks, and cars together, with Iranian technology and Venezuelan labor. They plan for steel companies and, of course, petroleum extraction ventures. In September 2006, the two leaders signed twenty-nine different agreements seeking to drive their respective—and somehow brotherly—revolutions forward.[87]

Perhaps the most famous and most threatening of the Iranian-Venezuelan cooperation schemes concerns Iran's nuclear ambitions, which Chávez wholeheartedly supports. He has announced that he would like to have nuclear reactors in Venezuela, and that he would bring this about with Iranian help. While the terrifying prospect of a nuclear Venezuela seems farther away than does a nuclear Iran, it would be such a dangerous proposition that we should not take it any more lightly. The recent support pledged by Russia to Chávez's nuclear ambitions may render Venezuela closer to nuclear capabilities than one would suspect.[88]

Though he hopes to receive nuclear aid from Iran, Chávez misses no opportunity to support Iran's own nuclear ambitions. In February 2006, the United Nations addressed the International Atomic Energy Agency's recommendation that Iran's uranium enrichment aims be brought before the Security Council. Venezuela was one of only three nations that voted against scrutinizing Iran. The other two: Cuba and Syria.[89] For his support of its nuclear program, the Iranian government bestowed on Chávez "the highest medal of the Islamic Republic of Iran."

Among the agreements the two nations have signed, there are some authorizing Iran to exploit Venezuelan minerals. There has been understandable and credible speculation that Venezuela is providing Iran with uranium for its nuclear program.[90] Naturally, it is very difficult to obtain hard evidence on this matter, though some respected newspapers report having had access to classified intelligence documents revealing that Venezuela does provide uranium to Iran.[91] During a hearing before the Subcommittee on International Terrorism and Nonproliferation of the Committee on International Relations of the U.S. House of Representatives, Congressman Edward R. Royce opened the session by reminding his audience that three years earlier "an intelligence official was quoted as saying, with respect to terrorism in Latin America, 'We don't even know what we don't know.'" Royce added, "I can't be sure that this has changed."[92]

Luckily, however, one need not be an intelligence official to put two and two together. Let us examine Chávez's relationship to terrorism with just a modicum of common sense. It is telling that prior to Chávez's regime, Venezuela had *never* been suspected of involvement with terrorist groups. The burden of proof has shifted. Chávez applauds terrorists and despises the United States, and the West in general, so the obvious question is: Why would Venezuela *not* ship uranium to Iran? Ahmadinejad is on the record about his desire to enrich uranium; Chávez is on the record supporting Iran's nuclear ambitions, as well as his own; they are both on the record professing almost erotic love for each other (in spite of their homophobic discourses). Perhaps Iran does not need Venezuela's uranium; perhaps it is just too cumbersome to transport it—even with all the new agreements between the two brotherly nations. In any case, it is frightening to contemplate that if he could, and if Ahmadinejad needed it, Chávez would gladly supply uranium or whatever else Ahmadinejad's nuclear ambitions demanded.

The same sort of reasonable inferences apply to Chávez's relationship with Hezbollah, Hamas, and other terrorist groups. As long as a group is anti-American or anti-Western, Chávez has supported it. One needn't even consider the large number of Venezuelans of Arab descent in Chávez's government, or his own exaltation of the noble Palestinian cause (which was also the struggle of Chávez's other "brother," Carlos the Jackal), or specific cases in which Venezuelan citizens of Arab descent have been accused by the United States of being Hezbollah agents. One need only listen to Chávez himself.

As Adam J. Szubin, the director of the Office of Foreign Assets Controls at the U.S. Department of the Treasury, remarked, "It is extremely troubling to see the Government of Venezuela employing and providing safe harbor to Hizballah facilitators and fundraisers."[93] The United States has, among other restrictions, frozen the assets of two Venezuelan travel agents (Ghazi Nasr Al Din and Fawzi Kan'an), one of whom has confirmed ties to Chávez's government, for actively financing and supporting Hezbollah.

The reasonable question again suggests itself: Why would Chávez *not* support these terrorist organizations? He is on the record expressing his admiration for them and their noble struggle; and they are on the record opposing the United States even more fanatically than Chávez does. As in the case of his relationship with Iran, I am uncertain as to the extent of Chávez's support, but it is more than reasonable to suspect that if he could, Chávez would help these organizations.

One would hope that other agencies of the United States government are as resolute as the Department of the Treasury has been, but we cannot be sure. For example, during the hearings just mentioned on Venezuela's relationship to terrorism, Congressman Brad Sherman made a statement in which he referred to Pat Robertson's imprudent call for Chávez's assassination:

> This issue, like almost everything concerning Venezuela these days, is potentially inflammatory or taken out of context. We need to be careful to ensure

that what we say here today provides no ammunition for those who want to paint America and our Congress as a caricature somehow of ugly Yankees who are opposed to the legitimate aims of the Venezuelan people for a prosperous democratic and fully independent country at peace with its neighbors and the world at large. This Committee is not the 700 Club. Pat Robertson is not here, and his remarks do not reflect the views of this Subcommittee, Congress, or the United States Government. This Subcommittee on International Terrorism and Nonproliferation is not concerned with Chávez's social policy or socialist ideology. The fact that, unfortunately, Mr. Chávez seems to look more to Marx than to Milton Friedman should concern the people of Venezuela but is not the concern of this Subcommittee.[94]

One need not endorse Pat Robertson's comments to see Congressman Sherman's exposition as misguided. Rather than investigating the many indicia pointing toward close ties between Chávez and terrorist groups, Sherman seemed perhaps too interested in reassuring Chávez's regime—and his fans in the United States—of the integrity and goodwill of the Subcommittee on International Terrorism and Nonproliferation. Sherman and his colleagues did ask some important questions and raise valuable points. For example, Sherman noted that "there is a Venezuelan citizen, Mr. Hakim Mamad al Diab Fatah, who attended school with the [9/11] hijackers"[95]—"the same flight school in New Jersey," in fact.[96] He said that the subcommittee had asked the Venezuelan government for cooperation in investigating this Venezuelan citizen, but "in every respect, the response is that the Venezuelan government won't even meet with our people."

The committee did ask about many of the suspicious activities of the Venezuelan government, with particular emphasis on U.S. "border vulnerabilities" in light of the fact that, as one *U.S. News* report of 2003 stated: "Thousands of Venezuelan identity documents are being distributed to foreigners from Middle Eastern nations, including Syria, Pakistan, Egypt, and Lebanon."[97] The danger posed by these Venezuelan identity documents can only increase now that "the government of Venezuela has signed a contract with the Cuban Ministry of Interior for the Cubans to run the Venezuelan office that issues documents, keeps records, [and] issues identity cards."[98]

Similarly, Congressman Jerry Weller asked about the fact that Chávez's government has purchased a number of assault rifles from Russia surpassing the number of people enlisted in the Venezuelan army, and that Venezuela has acquired the franchise to produce even larger numbers of these rifles in its own territory. But this deal pales in comparison with the other arms deals that Chávez has struck with Russia. He has already bought twenty-four Sukhoi fighter jets and missiles of different ranges from Russia[99]—a country he describes as "no empire" but rather a "great friend" of Venezuela.[100] Chávez's spending spree in Russia has reached such a level that the Russian president has stated that "Venezuela is now Russia's most important partner."[101] Chávez is in the process of buying submarines and sophisticated anti-aircraft batteries from Russia.[102] As if all these weapons were not enough, Chavez has even opened the doors to a Russian base on Venezuelan territory.[103]

In September 2008, in a blatant attempt to intimidate the United States, Russia sent two nuclear-arms-capable bombers to Venezuela for joint military exercises. This was "the first time Russian strategic bombers have landed in the Western Hemisphere since the Cold War."[104] In November 2008, Russia sent a naval squadron for more joint exercises with the Venezuelan navy.[105] This has been the first time that Russian ships have navigated the Caribbean since the Cold War.

Yet the official responses of the United States government seem tepid.[106] Gordon Johndroe, a National Security Council spokesman, simply said that Venezuela's offer to host a Russian fleet was "curious."[107] A couple of weeks before he "invited" the fleet to Venezuela, Chávez, on a visit to Russia, had in fact welcomed a Russian military base in his country.[108] Similarly, on his prepared statement for the congressional hearing on "Venezuela: Terrorism Hub of South America," Frank Urbancic Jr., the principal deputy coordinator at the Office of the Coordinator for Counterterrorism in the U.S. Department of State, affirmed that his office was increasing "efforts to expose Venezuela's out-of-step rhetoric and actions." But isn't referring to Chávez's rhetoric as "out-of-step" an understatement? During the same hearing, Congressman Royce explained the peculiar status that Venezuela had been assigned:

> In May, the State Department designated Venezuela as "not cooperating fully" with United States antiterrorism efforts. This designation is different than the more serious and commonly referred to state sponsor of terrorism designation. This designation precludes the sale of / licensing of defense material and services to Venezuela. Venezuela is now the only country on the "not cooperating fully" list that is not also designated as a state sponsor of terrorism.[109]

Congressman Royce suggested that "Venezuela is walking a thin line between 'not cooperating fully' against terrorism and 'state sponsorship' of terrorism."[110] Forget the thin lines: are not these delicately euphemistic discussions out of place? Leaving legalese aside, is it not rather obvious that Chávez truly is a very dangerous man?

THE CHÁVEZ LOBBY IN THE UNITED STATES

L obbyists of every stripe seek to persuade government officials to act in their clients' interests. There are almost as many lobbyists as there are powerful interests. Pharmaceutical companies, banks, automakers, and potential contractors with this or that local government all employ lobbyists. So, indeed, do countries, in order to advance their interests in other countries. Understandably, there tend to be more lobbyists working in powerful countries on behalf of less powerful countries than the other way around. Of course, a powerful country may find itself lobbying a less powerful one on a particular occasion—when it wishes to secure a contract or a concession of some sort. In general, however, more powerful countries simply do not need less powerful countries as much as vice versa. It is easy to see why the United States, a very powerful country, is a major hub for international lobbyists.

Lobbyists tend to have a bad reputation, as a result of the not entirely baseless suspicion that they often attain results via impermissible or otherwise objectionable means. Thus, a cottage industry of sorts has developed in the United States, devoted to denouncing international lobbyists and the havoc they supposedly wreak on the independence and autonomy of the country's foreign policy. While there are notorious lobbyists in the United States serving a large number of foreign nations, those lobbyists working on behalf of Israel, for example, are demonized with particular zeal and in especially strident tones.[1]

Not a word, however, is uttered about Chávez's lobby in the United States or in those Western countries he so fatuously antagonizes. Many, if not most, of my readers are doubtless hearing about the Chávez lobby for the first time. While Chávez's supporters talk of a United States misinformation campaign against the Chávez regime (recall Peter Coyote's talk of a "propaganda sandwich") and persist in presenting him as the victim of one and another defamatory effort, they seldom if ever provide evidence of any such campaign. Worse yet, they remain silent about the fact that it is Chávez who maintains a well-oiled global lobbying operation. At the very least, this silence reveals the two-facedness of Chávez's supporters.

To be sure, some of these supporters may be genuinely ignorant of the Chávez lobby's existence, but others are perfectly well aware of it. I will demonstrate that some of Chávez's supporters, indeed some of the ones whose falsehoods I have exposed in this book, have for years been in contact with Chávez's lobbyists.

For all I know, there is nothing illegal in the activities that I describe below. My goal is not to criticize lobbying as such, but to document the duplicity of both Chávez and many of his supporters. Whether or not some of their activities are immoral, and the extent to which the so-called Chávez experts are themselves part of his sophisticated and intense lobbying operation, I leave to my readers to decide.

Chávez's lobbyists cast a wide net. His regime funds *círculos bolivarianos* (Bolivarian Circles) in many countries.[2] But he also has more systematic means of advancing his agenda. He is influential in France through his friendship with Ignacio Ramonet, who controlled *Le Monde diplomatique* between 1991 and 2008. In the United Kingdom, Chávez can work through his alliance with Ken Livingstone, formerly the mayor of London, and through the Venezuela Information Centre[3] and the Venezuela Solidarity Campaign.[4] In Australia, there is the Australia-Venezuela Solidarity Network.[5] And so on, in many other countries. Chávez's lobbyists seemingly operate in cooperation with the Venezuelan government, as an Internet search or even a cursory look at the "Events" sections of their websites reveals: The Venezuelan embassies organize events, promote publications, and in effect launch and support the lucrative careers of many professional Chavistas.

In order to make my task somewhat manageable, however, I will restrict my efforts to accounting for a portion of Chávez's lobby activity within the United States. The Venezuelan regime puts vast amounts of petrodollars into paying scores of lobbyists; there are public documents, readily available online, recording these millions and millions of dollars. This suggests that he also spends money on lobbyists in other countries, like France, the United Kingdom, and Australia. If the Venezuela Information Office in the United States costs Chávez millions, would its British cousin, the Venezuela Information Centre, cost him nothing? I find it safe to assume that Chávez's lobbying operations in the United States are a model for analogous operations in other countries.

Most of my information about the Chávez lobby in the United States comes from documents available on a website that the Department of Justice maintains in accordance with the Foreign Agents Registration Act. These documents contain only that information which the lobbyists are legally required to disclose.[6] One can assume that the lobbyists disclose as little as possible; and the space allotted on the forms permits no more than a few words, though this is not the only conceivable explanation for the notably terse reports. I have no way of knowing whether the Chávez lobbyists report everything they ought to. I cannot be sure that all Chávez lobbyists (or quasi-lobbyists, etc.) are even registered. All the same, what *is* reported—even if it does not provide an exhaustive accounting of Chávez's operation in the United States—does at least point to how ambitious and systematic his efforts are. His lobbyists constitute a rather motley group: some of them are Washington insiders working for well-established and powerful law firms; others are environmentalist "heroes"; still others are members of the Black Panther Party, and so on.

Chávez has hired the lobbying and legal firm Patton Boggs LLP to help him give his image a "Washington make-over."[7] The firm describes itself on its website as follows: "Washington, D.C.-based Patton Boggs is a leader in Public Policy and Lobbying, Regulatory, Litigation, Business and Intellectual Property law." On the form that Patton Boggs submitted to the Department of Justice, it is stated that "some of the Registrant's [Patton Boggs's] activities may include public advocacy [i.e., lobbying] and public policy counseling, as well as interaction with officials from the Legislative and Executive Branches of Government."[8]

As the documents available at the Justice Department's website show, Patton Boggs's image-improvement services have cost Chávez several million dollars in the past few years. For example, Chávez agreed to pay Patton Boggs in excess of US $1,200,000 for a period of eleven and a half months in 2004.[9] Patton Boggs's fees the previous year were also well above a million dollars.[10] Similarly, early in his regime, Chávez entered into a contract with Arnold & Porter LLP, which provides for expenses of up to US $3,700,000 over a twelve-month period.[11]

Chávez also has a relationship with the Dutko Group LLC.[12] The "What We Do" section of Dutko's website suggests, in so many words, that the firm engages in lobbying activities: "In the public policy process, success requires victory in the campaign of ideas. Those who prevail utilize a range of techniques to convince others that they are right. Our job is to help them identify and leverage the tools needed to win."[13] The form that Dutko submitted to the Department of Justice is more explicit than its website: rather than hide behind euphemisms, it unapologetically uses the term "lobbying": "The Dutko Group LLC engages in general legislative lobbying with U.S. Federal Executive and Congressional offices. Lobbying is focused on increasing cooperation and economic investment in Venezuela. For this purpose, we seek to encourage U.S. government officials to visit Venezuela."[14] For their efforts, Chávez's government agreed to pay these lobbyists US $40,000 per month, plus expenses. Chávez's agreement with another firm, I Imagine Entertainment Inc., provides for US $35,000 per month plus expenses to "Write press releases, schedule press conferences, draft 'op ed' pieces for publication, and other public relations tactics."[15]

As noted before, not all of Chávez's lobbyists are merely business-oriented members of the Washington establishment. For example, Chávez contracted with Lumina Strategies LLC (US $60,000 for a three-month period, plus expenses). The firm declared that the activity for which they had been contracted by Chávez's regime was to "lobby for the Venezuelan government."[16] The president of Lumina Strategies, Michael Shellenberger, is presented on his own website as a champion of "clean energy." Indeed, he and a partner were named *Time* magazine's "Heroes of the Environment 2008."[17] Shellenberger is also described as being engaged in promoting "social values, national security and human rights."[18] Given what I have demonstrated about Chávez's regime, it is difficult to see why Shellenberger would agree to lobby for him. Chávez has also hired a Black Panther Party member, Leila McDowell[19] (US $5,000 per month), in order to have her "provide public relations counsel and assistance," "assist with oped placement," and "improve the image of the Republic of Venezuela."[20] The Venezuela Information Office LLC (henceforth, the VIO) also had a business relationship with the Gray Panthers.[21]

The list of lobbyists that Chávez has working for him in the United States is too long to present here in full, but these broad strokes should allow the outlines of the bigger picture to emerge. Very little seems to be shared by the motley assemblage of lobbyists that Chávez has put together—other than money. "Grab some of Chávez's money" seems to be the only operational motto they have in common, and Chávez certainly has tons of money and is only too happy to spend it on lobbyists.

Now, one may think that these sorts of activities are par for the course in the world of big business, and that it is understandable for any group, governmental or otherwise, to engage in them if its aim is success. Yet this rationalization becomes less palatable when one considers that Venezuela was more prosperous before Chávez seized power, but its lobbying activities were virtually nonexistent. One reason why Chávez's use of lobbyists is particularly problematic is that Chávez criticizes lobbyists in general while failing to mention that he has scores of them on his payroll. (His disdain for lobbyists is parroted by his supporters.)[22] A second reason is that Chávez's lobbyists do not merely seek to get this or that contract,[23] or to persuade this or that investor to put his money in Venezuela. Their main objective is to sell a falsified and sugarcoated image of Chávez and his regime. The targets of Chávez's lobbyists are often professors, students, and journalists.

For example, the Dutko Group's report of activities for July 2001, which it was required to file with the Department of Justice, admits that the group "prepared an op-ed article regarding the [Venezuelan] Ambassador's views and submitted it to the *Houston Chronicle*." Chávez's lobbyists at Dutko admit, furthermore, to having "worked with *Houston Chronicle* international affairs columnist Mae Ghalwash in her reporting of the ambassador's visit."[24] This instance of seemingly attempting to influence the news reporting of a supposedly independent major newspaper is but the tip of the iceberg; another group of Chávez's lobbyists has taken the practice of influencing the work of journalists, activists, and even congressmen and university professors to a truly shocking level.

The most active of all lobbyist groups for Chávez in the United States appears to be the VIO.[25] The website of this firm states that its goal is to "educate" and "present an accurate view of the current political scene in Venezuela for the American public." Interestingly, there is no "Who we are" section, or any information about specific funding sources other than a laconic note that "the VIO receives funding from the government of Venezuela." Documents submitted by the VIO to the Department of State (available on the latter's website), however, reveal that since 2004, some two dozen lobbyists have been on the

VIO's payroll, and that during this period Chávez has paid the VIO several million dollars.

Between May 19, 2004, and August 13, 2004, Chávez (via the Venezuelan embassy in Washington) gave US $500,000 to the VIO;[26] between October 20, 2004, and January 7, 2005, Chávez paid US $354,400 to the VIO;[27] between April 20, 2005, and July 19, 2005, he paid US $405,000;[28] between September 5, 2005, and January 17, 2006, he paid US $490,000;[29] between March 13, 2006, and July 20, 2006, he paid US $485,000;[30] on September 11, 2006, he paid US $325,000;[31] between April 30, 2007, and July 12, 2007, he paid US $755,000;[32] on January 22, 2008, he paid US $180,000;[33] and between April 19, 2008, and August 28, 2008, he paid US $814,000 to the VIO.[34] The information for certain months appears to be missing, but what we do have are records verifying that between May 19, 2004, and August 2008, Chávez paid the VIO at least US $4,308,400.

And how do these lobbyists spend the Venezuelan money that Chávez so wastefully—though to the applause of his many supporters—throws at them? Some activities are not easy to determine, since the VIO actually subcontracts (this is the term used in the official documents) some tasks. Consider the isolated example of Segundo Mercado-Llorens, a Washington lobbyist[35] subcontracted by the VIO. Records shows that at some point during the six-month period ending on August 31, 2005, Chávez's lobbyists at the VIO paid Segundo Mercado-Llorens US $70,000;[36] during the six-month period ending on February 28, 2006, Chávez's lobbyists paid him US $60,000;[37] during the six-month period ending on August 31, 2006, they paid him US $60,000;[38] during the six-month period ending on February 28, 2007, they paid him US $90,000;[39] during the six-month period ending on August 31, 2007, they paid him US $30,000.[40] From the documents available at the Department of Justice, it is not possible to determine what Mercado-Llorens did with the US $310,000 he was paid over the course of these two years.

Those activities which VIO does not subcontract are somewhat easier to track. Numerous and varied though they are, these activities generally concern improving Chávez's public image and ruining the image of anyone critical of him. For instance, after Mary Anastasia O'Grady wrote in the *Wall Street Journal* about Chávez's relationship with Patton Boggs—which to my knowledge was how it first came to public attention—the VIO sought diligently to discredit O'Grady. They produced a hit piece on her, which they distributed widely and eventually published in various venues, including the website of Gregory Wilpert, one of the "experts" on Chávez whom I discussed above (and whose connections to the VIO I will detail below).

VIO lobbyists regularly talk with journalists; indeed, they canvass many of the most influential newspapers and magazines in the United States. On November 22, 2004, Chávez's lobbyists at the VIO reported having contacted thirty-two people, requesting their responses to a *Washington Post* editorial, "Watch Venezuela," which appeared on November 20. It is hard to imagine that these requests were not backed by assurances of publication or perhaps other enticements. On December 1, VIO lobbyists contacted the editors of a dozen newspapers "pitching ideas for editorials," and on subsequent days they followed up with many of these editors.[41] The documents at the Department of Justice reveal that VIO lobbyists are particularly active in reacting to anything that comments on Chávez's regime with less than glowing praise, as the case of the *Wall Street Journal's* O'Grady reveals. Similarly, the *Washington Post* reported that after PBS aired a rather even-handed documentary about Chávez on *Frontline,* the VIO "encouraged its supporters to complain about the Frontline program." The producer of the documentary, Ofra Bikel, called the VIO's complaint "baseless."[42]

VIO lobbyists' interests are not limited to members of the press. Peter Camejo of the Green Party, formerly the vice-presidential candidate on Ralph Nader's ticket, was contacted by the VIO on October 10, 2006, in hopes that he would "write an oped on Venezuela." Mark

Weisbrot, from the Center for Economic Policy and Research,[43] is often contacted by VIO lobbyists; for instance, on August 27, 2007, he was asked by the VIO about "writing a letter to the editor." Also contacted often is Laura Safer Espinoza, an "acting justice" on the New York State Supreme Court; on November 15, 2007, VIO requested that she "submit oped pieces to local papers."[44] And these VIO efforts seem to be effective, for those contacted tend to write favorably about Chávez.[45]

The list of people contacted by VIO lobbyists is extensive, including hundreds of names. Some are famous personalities, such as Howard Zinn (Harvard University) and Noam "Chompsky [sic]" (Massachusetts Institute of Technology), Ed Asner, Naomi Klein, John Pilger, Roger Toussaint (New York Transportation Workers Union), and Jennifer McCoy (Carter Center); others are less-known people like Angelo Rivero-Santos (Georgetown University), August Nimtz (University of Minnesota), Mark Becker (Truman State University), Emelio Betances (Gettysburg College), and Fernando Coronil (University of Michigan). The VIO has even contacted virtual unknowns, such as students at various universities and many of the beneficiaries of Chávez's cheap heating oil program, in order to discuss their potential participation in "a delegation to Venezuela to the [sic] discuss heating oil program with civil society and government circles." Again, this information is public and is available on the website of the Department of Justice, and when I quote, I am quoting from the official documents contained therein.[46]

Sometimes the VIO reports merely acknowledge having met with so and so on one or two occasions. In other cases, the VIO and these individuals appear to be in more frequent contact. Consider some reported highlights of the case of Jennifer Wager, the director of *Venezuela Rising,* a pro-Chávez documentary that "has screened at film festivals around the world," according to her website.[47] Wager was contacted by the VIO on October 28, 2004, regarding "Outreach for documentary." When she was contacted on March 10, 2006, the report notes that she "Will provide DVD to VIO at cost." On March 31, she was contacted about "Permission to reproduce documentary." A couple of weeks later, the VIO was showing Ms. Wager's film at events it sponsored across the United States—for instance, at an event "commemorating the Fourth Anniversary of the Return of Democracy to Venezuela," which took place on April 13, 2006, in the Festival Center in Washington, D.C. (The event also included a "panel discussion" between Mark Weisbrot and Edward Mercado, a lobbyist from the VIO.) Apparently the VIO could not get enough of Ms. Wager's DVDs: On October 30, 2006, she was contacted again with a request to "send more DVDs or make copies." On December 13, 2007, she was asked to "attend [an] event in [the] Bronx." On March 11, 2008, she was asked to "meet with activists." On March 20, 2008, she was asked to "attend and make comment" at a "human rights event."[48] While there is perhaps nothing objectionable about Ms. Wager's behavior, one interpretation of her repeated contact with the VIO, which in fact is an important buyer and distributor of her work, is that it casts doubt on that work's independence and autonomy.

Also instructive are highlights of the interaction between VIO lobbyists and Maria Campos-Brito, whom the VIO lists as affiliated with Loyola University. On September 13, 2007, VIO lobbyists invited Campos-Brito to "participate in a public event" on the occasion of the "Presidential Visit to NYC." She was contacted again by another VIO lobbyist on September 27, 2007; the report described the "Position Advocated" on this occasion as "stay in touch on research." Barely a month later, on October 24, Campos-Brito was contacted again by VIO lobbyists, this time so she would "write an OpEd on Venezuela's referendum on the constitutional reform." On December 11, 2007, she was invited to "Attend the Venezuelan Heating Oil Program event in DC." Again, given this sort of interaction between Campos-Brito and VIO lobbyists, it is hard to imagine that she is independent of or indifferent to the VIO's concerns and agenda.

Perhaps more significant are VIO lobbyists' contacts with members of the United States Congress. For example, on March 5, 2004, lobbyists "stopped by" the offices of some two dozen U.S. senators in order to discuss "democracy; nonintervention" in Venezuela. In subsequent days they met with a number of legislative aides to members of Congress. This sort of contact is reported very frequently in the forms that the VIO has submitted to the Department of Justice.[49]

One case is particularly interesting: that of José Serrano, a representative from the 16th Circuit of New York. VIO lobbyists report having contacted Congressman Serrano's office no fewer than five times in September 2004. On December 6 of that year, they faxed "educational materials" dealing with the alleged "CIA knowledge of coup d'état" to a group of representatives in Congress.[50]

Two days later, Serrano issued a press release: "Newly Declassified CIA Documents Show Blatant Administration Deception During Coup, Raise Serious Questions about the Administration's Judgment and Commitment to Veracity." The press release is highly critical of the United States government's manner of dealing with Chávez.[51] Serrano's language and tone are very similar to those used by VIO lobbyists themselves in the pro-Chávez literature that they regularly disseminate (also available at the Justice Department's website).[52] This should surprise no one, since the most prominent source listed in Serrano's release was none other than Eva Golinger's website (www.venezuelafoia.info). On its face, the press release relies heavily on the work of a strong supporter of Chávez and Chávez's lobbyists.

On the same day that Congressman Serrano issued his press release, Ben Allen, listed as his press secretary, received an email and a phone call from VIO lobbyists, the contents of which were summarized as follows: "Interesting statement: demonstrates commitment to democracy in hemisphere."[53]

Rather than present more highlights of the myriad contacts and activities of the VIO's lobbyists in general, I would like to focus on the contacts between VIO lobbyists and some of those so-called experts on Chávez whose views I have criticized in this book. I intend to demonstrate that Julia Buxton, Charles Hardy, Bart Jones, and Gregory Wilpert, whose books I have shown to be significantly flawed, have been in direct contact with VIO lobbyists over the years. So too have Steve Ellner and Dan Hellinger, who edited a book titled *Venezuelan Politics in the Chávez Era.*

The documentation shows that Buxton has been regularly contacted by VIO lobbyists so as to exchange information and distribute material concerning Chávez's Venezuela, and that she has had some of her work distributed by those very lobbyists. For example, on April 26, 2005, lobbyists emailed "Prof. Julia Buxton's reply to Michael Shifter's 04/07 op-ed in FT on Venezuela" to some fifty journalists. On March 6, 2007, Buxton, then a visiting professor at Georgetown University, was contacted by a VIO lobbyist and asked to "hold a meeting on Venezuela." On May 1, 2007, she was contacted again and "asked about a letter to the editor." On May 24, 2007, VIO lobbyists again contacted her (together with Steve Ellner and others), inquiring about her "availability for comment on RCTV." On September 14, 2007, lobbyists contacted Julia Buxton, asking her to "write a response" to "Phil Gunson article on Chavez."[54] Does the VIO ask that these things be done for free, one wonders?

Documents indicate that Steve Ellner was contacted in September 2004 and asked to discuss a "large Forum on Racism in Venezuela." When he was contacted again on November 18, 2004, the "Position Advocated" section of the document submitted to the Department of Justice was filled out this way: "Strengthening support networks and educating the public on Venezuela's position on the FFTA." On March 9, 2005, Steve Ellner met with a VIO lobbyist; the "Position Advocated" was "Distribute papers on his research." Between June 8 and June 11, 2005, a VIO lobbyist spoke on the phone with some two dozen people, in order to discuss their participation in a session to be broadcast by one of Chávez's television stations, Telesur. On March 9, 2006, Ellner was contacted so that he would "Speak at hill briefing." On September 5, 2007, Ellner was contacted via email and asked to "give a lecture on Venezuela's labor movement." On January 15, 2008,

Ellner was contacted by VIO lobbyists; the "Position Advocated" was "publicize book." On April 4, 2008, he was invited to "give lectures in DC."[55]

Documents show that on October 19, 2007, a lobbyist contacted Charles Hardy requesting that he discuss a delegation to Venezuela and asking him to "help set up a meeting with Bolivarian University," one of the new "universities" that Chávez has created by decree in Venezuela. On March 12, 2007, another VIO lobbyist contacted Hardy asking him if he would be available to speak in Washington, D.C. On June 6, 2007, Hardy, Steve Ellner, and Jim Green were contacted by lobbyists wondering whether "[we] can . . . include you as a press contact in press release [?]." On August 22, 2007, Hardy was contacted and "asked for copies of a book on Venezuela." On March 7, 2008, he was contacted again and asked to "link to VenWorld blog [from his own website]."

According to the documentation, on August 24, 2005, Dan Hellinger was invited by VIO lobbyists to "promote his understanding of the Venezuela human rights situation at St Louis public event." On January 27, 2006, he was contacted again by a lobbyist from the VIO; the "Position Advanced" was "Preparation for lobby day." On February 16, 2007, Hellinger was contacted to "do radio interview." On March 14, 2006, the request was to "Speak at hill briefing." On January 24, 2008, a VIO lobbyist "suggested ideas for research." On August 11, 2008, Hellinger was asked to "travel to Venezuela" and to "use VIO contacts."[56]

Documents show that on April 2, 2004, Bart Jones was contacted by VIO lobbyists; the "Position Advocated" in the form is "Good article." He was contacted again regarding a variety of issues on April 22, May 25, and June 23. On November 29 that year, Jones informed of "CIA knowledge of the coup." (Around this time, VIO lobbyists were also busy persuading congressmen of the same, as we saw above.) On February 22, 2006, Jones was "offered feedback on interview." On May 31,

2007, he was "asked about writing a letter to the editor." On August 28, 2007, he was "asked for promo material on Chávez biography."[57]

Documents show that Gregory Wilpert has also been contacted often, on a variety of matters, including to request that he link to the VIO's website on his ostensibly impartial (though blatantly pro-Chávez) website. On August 14, 2007, he was "asked that articles on Venezuela be posted" on his website. On December 17, 2007, he was asked by one of the VIO's lobbyists to "meet with delegation of Colorado University School of Public Health to discuss Venezuela's health care system." On April 14, 2008, he was asked to "link [his website] to VenWorld blog."[58]

Earlier, I noted that aside from Islamic fundamentalists, no other religious or quasi-religious group is as excited about Chávez's farcical revolution as the Maryknoll religious order. Charles Hardy and Bart Jones have been associated with Maryknoll, and we have seen how closely they have worked with Chávez's lobbyists. But they are not the only Maryknoll-related people in contact with the VIO. Roy Bourgeois, currently fighting excommunication from the Catholic Church, has also been invited—together with several of his colleagues at Pax Christi and at School of the Americas Watch—to "work with VIO" in a variety of capacities. Another Maryknoll lay missionary, David Kane, was invited on June 10, 2005, to participate in a television show on Telesur.[59]

Documents show that Lisa Sullivan, another Maryknoll lay missionary, has been in such regular contact with VIO lobbyists that it has been speculated that she "work[s] for Venezuela Information Center in Washington."[60] On January 11, 2005, Sullivan—together with Marie Dennis, the director of Maryknoll's Office for Global Concerns—was contacted by VIO lobbyists to discuss "Coordination for delegation to Venezuela." Sullivan and Dennis were contacted by the VIO again on January 28, 2005, and invited to have "Breakfast with Vice Minister Hernandez." On April 10, 2005, Sullivan was invited to "write article on her experiences working with Venezuela's poor." On March 8, 2007, Sullivan was requested to "ask religious groups for support" in connection with an "Interfaith Conference on Venezuela." On September 18, 2007, she was asked by the VIO to offer "services as an interpreter for the SEIU delegation to Venezuela." On October 19, 2007, she was sent two different emails by VIO lobbyists: one in which she was asked to "identify Venezuelans to speak" and another in which she was invited to "have religious letter sent to Congress." All in all, according to official reports, Lisa Sullivan has been contacted by VIO lobbyists at least thirty times since 2005.[61] Perhaps those who claim that she works for the VIO are on to something.

I believe that the reports the VIO is legally required to submit to the Department of Justice suggest an easily recognizable pattern. It is difficult to imagine that the errors I have pointed out in the books of Charles Hardy and Bart Jones and Gregory Wilpert, among others, are simply the result of ignorance or incompetence. Those errors may well have more to do with the authors' rather frequent contacts with the salaried lobbyists of Chávez's regime. The reports are evidence that VIO lobbyists are paid by the Venezuelan government—and paid to disseminate what I have attempted to reveal as a prefabricated version of Venezuelan history and of Chávez's regime. That version is fundamentally, and often absurdly, false. Whether Chávez's panegyrists, some of whom teach at universities and present their work as if it were scholarship, are also being compensated by Chávez's government is an issue that I leave for my readers to assess. What appears beyond doubt is that these authors belong to a network that includes Chávez's salaried lobbyists and officials of his regime.

Describing Chávez as a hypocrite is an understatement. After all, he claims to hate the "evil empire" of the United States, but spends fortunes doing business and cultivating a positive image there. That Chávez is much worse than a mere hypocrite I hope to have demonstrated in this book, but I want to conclude with some reflections on the work of Chávez's lobbyists.

First, in addition to its incessant efforts to glorify Chávez's regime, the VIO often organizes delegations to visit Venezuela, or to meet with

Venezuelan officials visiting the United States. Often these delegations include ordinary Americans who (foolishly) feel gratitude to Chávez for his (self-serving) cheap oil schemes, or who have simply been gulled by the sorts of texts disseminated by Chávez's lobbyists. But in many cases these delegations are not composed strictly of the naïve and misinformed.

One telling but hardly isolated example is the international "observers" who were certified by the Venezuelan Electoral Council (the same council whose chairman left the post when Chávez appointed him vice president of Venezuela) to oversee the elections of December 3, 2006. The overwhelming majority of these observers were contacted, and presumably selected, if not by VIO lobbyists, at least with their input. In the circumstances, the observers' credibility appears suspect.

Among these observers, I will focus on a group of four "experts" (also called "leading U.S. academic and political experts" in VIO documents): Miguel Tinker-Salas, Dan Hellinger, Ricardo Moreno, and Mark Weisbrot. Three of these "experts" had been in contact with the VIO, as anyone can verify by examining the documents available through the Department of Justice.[62] The fourth "expert," Ricardo Moreno, was himself the executive director of the VIO—in other words, a lobbyist, paid by Chávez's government.[63] On the occasion of yet another of Chávez's elections, on September 14, 2007, VIO lobbyists contacted Eva Golinger, herself a close collaborator with the VIO and various other pro-Chávez lobbying organizations (and the main source for Congressman Serrano's above-mentioned press release). The VIO asked Golinger to "suggest lawyers for delegation."[64]

What can be said about the integrity of such delegations and of the elections that they were supposed to monitor? Not much, I am afraid.

A second point about Chávez's lobbyists is one that reflects on the United States. For all the criticism of other lobbyists—say, Israel's— Chávez's lobby is much more dangerous. Let us suppose, hypothetically, that the Israel lobby is a bad thing—that lobbyists working for

Israel manage to affect United States policy in ways that permit immoral or illegal conduct on Israel's part. Now, the foreign policy of Israel, as that of any other country on earth, includes its fair share of errors as well as successes. But one thing that is likely impossible to show about Israeli foreign policy is that it demonstrates true animosity toward the United States. Thus, by allowing the lobbying on behalf of Israel to continue, the United States would, at worst, be exaggerating its support for a friendly nation.

Chávez's Venezuela, by contrast, is an outspoken enemy of the United States, yet it carries out an ambitious lobbying operation there with impunity, while critics of lobbyism in general maintain a deafening silence on Chávez's lobby. And why is a sworn enemy of the United States even permitted to operate within its territory? Chávez is, after all, on the record expressing his desire to "bring down" and "destroy" the "decadent," "evil" United States. It is one thing to allow friendly nations like Israel (or neutral ones like Finland or Costa Rica) to lobby within your own territory; it is a very different thing to allow an avowed enemy, like Chávez's Venezuela, to do so.

The Department of Justice collects the documents from which I have constructed the bulk of this appendix because submitting these documents is mandated by the Foreign Agents Registration Act.[65] This law was passed in 1938, on the eve of the Second World War, as a response to Nazi Germany's attempts to carry out espionage and propaganda campaigns within the United States. Since 1938, then, any person who represents the interests of a foreign nation (or "principal") is required to register his or her activities with the Department of Justice. But should not the United States government do something about the information it collects?

NOTES

Chapter One: Venezuela and Its History

[1] Any list would be incomplete, but some prominent examples of this disdain for the historical background to Chávez are: Julia Buxton, *The Failure of Political Reform in Venezuela* (Aldershot, UK: Ashgate, 2001); Bart Jones, *¡Hugo! The Hugo Chávez Story from Mud Hut to Perpetual Revolution* (Hanover, N.H.: Steerforth Press, 2007); Richard Gott, *In the Shadow of the Liberator: Hugo Chávez and the Transformation of Venezuela* (London: Verso, 2000); Aleida Guevara, *Hugo Chavez and the New Latin America: An Interview with Hugo Chávez* (New York: Ocean Press, 2005); Charles Hardy, *Cowboy in Caracas: A North American's Memoir of Venezuela's Democratic Revolution* (Willimantic, Conn.: Curbstone Press, 2007); Eva Golinger, *The Chávez Code: Cracking U.S. Intervention in Venezuela* (Northampton, Mass.: Olive Branch Press, 2006); Eva Golinger, *Bush versus Chávez: Washington's War on Venezuela* (New York: Monthly Review Press, 2008); Tariq Ali, *Pirates of the Caribbean: Axis of Hope* (London: Verso, 2006); and Gregory Wilpert, *Changing Venezuela by Taking Power: The History and Politics of the Chávez Government* (London: Verso, 2007). Even balanced books, like Cristina Marcano and Alberto Barrera Tyszka's *Hugo Chávez: The Definitive Biography of Venezuela's Controversial President* (New York: Random House, 2004), or Rossana Miranda and Luca Mastrantonio's *Hugo Chávez: Il Caudillo Pop* (Venice: Marsilio Editori, 2007), contain very little by way of historical background.

[2] John Lynch, *Simón Bolívar: A Life* (New Haven: Yale University Press, 2006), p. 3.

[3] Manuel Rodríguez Campos, ed., *Diccionario de Historia de Venezuela*, 2nd ed. (Caracas: Fundación Polar, 1997), vol. 4, p. 586.

[4] Jose de Oviedo y Baños, *Historia de la Conquista y Población de la Provincia de Venezuela*, ed. Tomás Eloy Martínez (Caracas: Biblioteca Ayacucho, 1992), pp. 248–49.

[5] Mariano Picón Salas, "Venezuela: Algunas Gentes y Libros" in Mariano Picón Salas, Augusto Mijares, et al., *Venezuela Independiente: 1810–1960* (Caracas: Fundación Eugenio Mendoza, 1962), p. 7.

[6] John Lynch, *Simón Bolívar: A Life*, p. 8.

[7] These volumes are stored in Venezuela's *Academia Nacional de la Historia*.

[8] Andrés Bello, *Obras Completas* (Caracas: La Casa de Bello, 1981–1984).

[9] Rafael Caldera, *Andrés Bello: Philosopher, Poet, Philologist, Educator, Jurist, Statesman* (London: Allen & Unwin, 1977). Rafael Caldera played an important role in Chávez's ascent to power.

[10] Andrés Eloy Blanco, "Clase," in his *Obras Completas* (Caracas: Ediciónes del Congreso de la República, 1973). Fittingly, Blanco himself died in exile in 1955, in México City, during one of Venezuela's many dictatorships.

[11] Manuel Rodríguez Campos, ed., *Diccionario de Historia de Venezuela*, 2nd ed. (Caracas: Fundación Polar, 1997), vol. 1, p. 478.

[12] This is at the beginning of a chapter titled "Mental Characteristics." J. L. Salcedo Bastardo, *Visión y Revisión de Bolívar* (Caracas: Ediciónes del Ministerio de Educación, 1960), p. 77.

[13] In a chapter titled "Moral Figure [of Bolívar]." Ibid., p. 89.

[14] Ibid., p. 67.

[15] José Rafael Pocaterra, *Memorias de un Venezolano de la Decadencia* (Caracas: Elite, 1936), vol. 1, p. 103. Pocaterra was the Venezuelan ambassador to the United States from 1949 to 1950.

[16] Germán Carrera Damas, *El Culto a Bolívar* (Caracas: Grijalbo, 1989); Luis Castro Leiva, "De la Patria Boba a la Teología Bolivariana," in *Luis Castro Leiva: Obras*, ed. Carole Leal Curiel (Caracas: Fundación Polar, 2005).

[17] Contrast my view with that of, for example, José Sant Roz, in his *Bolívar y Chávez* (Merida: Fuerza Bolivariana de la Universidad de Los Andes,

2003), who argues that the two men are almost identical. Sant Roz's book has been financed and published by Chávez's government.

[18] For more on racial attitudes throughout Venezuelan history, see, e.g., Winthrop R. Wright, *Café con Leche: Race, Class, and National Image in Venezuela* (Austin: University of Texas Press, 1990).

[19] See the notice from the Venezuelan Ministry of Foreign Relations: http://www.mre.gov.ve/Noticias/Viceministros/Vice-Africa/A2008/Declar-093a.htm, April 15, 2008.

[20] See: http://www.youtube.com/watch?v=_TBAWpzhdSM, March 21, 2008.

[21] See: http://www.vicepresidencia.gov.ve/marcoh.asp, March 21, 2008.

[22] See: http://www.eluniversal.com.mx/notas/478259.html, March 21, 2008.

[23] See: http://www.eluniversal.com/2007/12/17/pol_ava_Chávez-ordeno-abrir_17A1264609.shtml, March 21, 2008.

[24] Ibid.

[25] John Lynch, *Simón Bolívar: A Life*, p. 245; and see also the references on p. 328.

[26] For brief introductions to Bentham's utilitarianism see Jeremy Bentham, *An Introduction to the Principles of Morals and Legislation* (New York: Haffner Press, 1973). For Mill's version of utilitarianism, see John Stuart Mill, *Utilitarianism*, ed. George Sher (Indianapolis: Hackett, 2001). The most cogent attack on classical liberalism is found in G. E. Moore, *Principia Ethica*, ed. Thomas Baldwin (Cambridge: Cambridge University Press, 2000), but there are countless contemporary contributions that highlight the many problems with Benthamite utilitarianism.

[27] Chávez repeats the phrase on a regular basis, so much so that it has become some sort of capsule of his entire political worldview. See: http://www.minci.gov.ve/noticias-prensa-presidencial/28/10296/revolucion_bolivariana_continua.html, March 21, 2008.

[28] Simón Bolívar, *Discurso de Angostura*, in *Doctrina del Libertador*, ed. Manuel Pérez Vila (Caracas: Biblioteca Ayacucho, 1976), p. 94. These remarks are dated February 15, 1819.

[29] Ibid., p. 65.

30 Ibid., p. 64.

31 Ibid., p. 65.

32 John Lynch, *Simón Bolívar: A Life*, p. 153.

33 Ibid., pp. 217–18.

34 Gregory Wilpert, *Changing Venezuela by Taking Power: The History and Politics of the Chávez Government* (London: Verso, 2007), p. 16.

35 Bart Jones, *¡Hugo! The Hugo Chávez Story from Mud Hut to Perpetual Revolution* (Hanover, N.H.: Steerforth Press, 2007), p. 47.

36 Read it all in "Venezuelan Embassy Hosts Solidarity Discussion," available here: http://www.greenleft.org.au/2007/717/37233.

37 Gustavus Hippisley, *A Narrative of the Expedition to the Rivers Orinoco and Apuré in South America; Which Sailed from England in November 1817, and Joined the Patriotic Forces in Venezuela and Caraccas* (London: John Murray, 1819); and, Henry La Fayette Villaume Ducoudray Holstein, *Memoirs of Simon Bolivar, President Liberator of the Republic of Colombia; and of His Principal Generals; Secret History of the Revolution, and the Events which Preceded It, from 1807 to the Present Time* (Boston: S. G. Goodrich, 1829).

38 Gustavus Hippisley, *A Narrative of the Expedition to the Rivers Orinoco and Apuré*, pp. 461–63.

39 Ducoudray Holstein, *Memoirs of Simon Bolivar*, pp. 324–25.

40 John Lynch, *Simón Bolívar: A Life*, p. 77.

41 Ibid., p. 124.

42 In a somewhat obscure piece, titled "La Hamaca de Bolívar" (Bolívar's Hammock), Arturo Uslar Pietri mentions both Hippisley and Ducoudray Holstein, but only to criticize them for failing to understand the cultural significance of the hammock. Given all the charges that Hippisley and Ducoudray Holstein raise against Bolívar, the fact that he liked to rest on his hammock is rather unimportant. See Arturo Uslar Pietri, "La Hamaca de Bolívar," in *Bolívar Hoy* (Caracas: Monte Avila, 1983).

43 John Lynch, *Simón Bolívar: A Life*, p. 314. Technically speaking, the name of the country was changed via constitutional reform. But the reform and the name change had been Chávez's vehement demand.

44 Karl Marx and Frederick Engels, *Collected Works*, vol. 40 (New York: International Publishers, 1983), p. 266. Marx's words, lest it be thought that

the translator exaggerated, are equally extreme in the original German: *"Den feigsten, gemeinsten, elendesten Lump als Napoleon I. verschrien zu sehn, war etwas zu toll. Bolívar ist der wahre Soulouque."* Karl Marx and Friedrich Engels, *Werke*, vol. 29 (Berlin: Dietz Verlag, 1973), p. 280.

45 The editors from the USSR's Institute of Marxism-Leninism attempted to soften the blow by suggesting that all Marx had available were the books by Hippisley and Ducoudray Holstein, and that these books were "biased." Poor Karl had been fooled. See, e.g., Karl Marx and Frederick Engels, *Collected Works*, vol. 40, p. 614, n. 282.

46 Guillermo Morón, *Breve Historia Contemporanea de Venezuela* (México: Fondo de Cultura Económica, 1994), p. 171.

47 Simón Bolívar, *Manifiesto de Cartagena*, in *Doctrina del Libertador*, ed. Manuel Pérez Vila (Caracas: Biblioteca Ayacucho, 1994), p. 7ff.

48 Ibid., p. 10.

49 Simón Bolívar, *Discurso de Angostura*, in *Doctrina del Libertador*, p. 90.

50 Ibid., p. 91.

51 Simón Bolívar, *Doctrina del Libertador*, p. 230ff.

52 Ducoudray Holstein, *Memoirs of Simon Bolivar*, p. 57.

53 Simón Bolívar, *Doctrina del Libertador*, p. 88.

54 Pedro León Zapata, *El Chávez de Zapata* (Caracas: Los Libros de El Nacional, 2002), p. 109.

55 Robert J. Alexander, *The Venezuelan Democratic Revolution: A Profile of the Regime of Rómulo Betancourt* (New Brunswick: Rutgers University Press, 1964).

56 Ibid., p. viii.

57 Ibid., p. vii.

58 Incidentally, Chávez wishes to create an Organization of American States that would exclude the United States and Canada. He has presented this exclusionary proposal repeatedly (although rarely does he mention Canada as a country to be excluded); for one example, see his speech of April 13, 2008, briefly noted by the Venezuelan Ministry of Information here: http://www.rnv.gov.ve/noticias/index.php?act=ST&f=2&t=65191.

59 As Mario Vargas Llosa has noted, "the most wise and sensible members of the Venezuelan intelligentsia, be they left-leaning, right-leaning, or centrist,

oppose Chávez's tyrannical regime." Read his whole article "El poder y el delirio" ("Power and Delirium") for *El País* here: http://www.elpais. com/articulo/opinion/poder/delirio/elpepiopi/20081214elpepiopi_13/Tes.

[60] Nikolas Kozloff, *Hugo Chávez: Oil, Politics, and the Challenge to the United States* (New York: Palgrave Macmillan, 2006), p. 61.

[61] María Pilar García-Guadilla, "Civil Society: Institutionalization, Fragmentation, Autonomy," in *Venezuelan Politics in the Chávez Era: Class, Polarization, and Conflict,* ed. Steve Ellner and Daniel Hellinger (London: Boulder, 2003), p. 179.

[62] D. L. Raby, *Democracy and Revolution: Latin America and Socialism Today* (London: Pluto Press, 2006), p. 135.

[63] Richard Gott, *In the Shadow of the Liberator: Hugo Chávez and the Transformation of Venezuela* (London: Verso, 2000), p. 17.

[64] Julia Buxton, *The Failure of Political Reform in Venezuela* (Aldershot, UK: Ashgate, 2001), p. 19.

[65] Ibid., p. 31.

[66] Guillermo Morón, *Breve Historia Contemporanea de Venezuela,* p. 287.

[67] See, e.g., the text of the pact in Haydee Miranda Bastidas, Hasdrúbal Becerra, and David Ruiz Chataing, eds., *Documentos Fundamentales de La Historia de Venezuela: 1777–1993* (Caracas: Los Libros de El Nacional, 1999), pp. 174–79.

Chapter Two: Hugo Chávez, the Man and His Reign

[1] See, e.g., Bart Jones, *¡Hugo! The Hugo Chávez Story from Mud Hut to Perpetual Revolution* (Hanover, N.H.: Steerforth Press, 2007); Charles Hardy, *Cowboy in Caracas: A North American's Memoir of Venezuela's Democratic Revolution* (Willimantic, Conn.: Curbstone Press, 2007); Richard Gott, *In the Shadow of the Liberator: Hugo Chávez and the Transformation of Venezuela* (London: Verso, 2000).

[2] Charles Hardy, *Cowboy in Caracas,* p. 93.

[3] Hugo Chávez Frías, *Venezuela del 04F-92 al 06D-98: Habla el Comandante Hugo Chávez Frías,* interview by Agustín Blanco Muñoz (Caracas: Cátedra Pio Tamayo, 1998), p. 35.

[4] Ibid.

[5] Ibid.

6 See Cristina Marcano and Alberto Barrera Tyszka, *Hugo Chávez: The Definitive Biography of Venezuela's Controversial President* (New York: Random House, 2004), unnumbered photographs.

7 Hugo Chávez Frías, *Habla el Comandante*, p. 36.

8 Ibid., p. 37.

9 See the devastating critique by José Ignacio Cabrujas in "La Lengua de la Juez Cabrera," *El Pais según Cabrujas* (Caracas: Monteavila/El Diario de Caracas, 1992), pp. 153–57.

10 See Agustín Blanco Muñoz, *Habla Herma Marskman: Hugo Chávez me Utilizó* (Caracas: Cátedra Pio Tamayo, 2004).

11 Bart Jones, *¡Hugo! The Hugo Chávez Story*, p. 180.

12 Ibid., p. 472.

13 Ibid., p. 180.

14 See, e.g., http://www.timesonline.co.uk/tol/news/world/article1083077.ece.

15 See, e.g., Reiner Luyken, "Der Narziss von Caracas," *Die Zeit* 43 (2002), available here: http://www.zeit.de/2002/43/Der_Narziss_von_Caracas. Also, Andrés Oppenheimer, *Cuentos Chinos: El engaño de Washington, la mentira populista y la esperanza de América Latina* (Caracas: Random House Mondadori, 2005), p. 223.

16 See the report about it in Argentina's newspaper *El Clarin*: http://www.clarin.com/diario/2003/08/17/p-01201.htm.

17 The biblical story is in I Kings 3:16–28. See Chávez's performance here: http://www.youtube.com/watch?v=DLRwcSHbFbc.

18 See, e.g., http://www.youtube.com/watch?v=Ad-ppoprQTw&NR=1.

19 See, e.g., http://news.bbc.co.uk/2/hi/americas/7090600.stm. The BBC did not report the whole thing. For a full account of Chávez's words, see Camilo Chaparro, "*El que me acusa de dictador es un ignorante*": Frases de *Hugo Chávez* (Bogota: Intermedio, 2007), p. 97. The title of the book in English would be "He Who Accuses Me of Being a Dictator Is an Ignoramus: Hugo Chávez's Phrases"; and it is just that—a list of Chávez's favorite sayings. The one chosen for the title speaks volumes about Chávez's argumentative habits.

20 The expression in Spanish is "*Vayase al carajo*," which is stronger than "go to hell," although this is the closest translation: http://www.youtube.com/watch?v=TNSwJN1_ZrE.

[21] See the documentary *The Well-Oiled Revolution of Hugo Chávez,* produced by the Netherland Public Broadcasting. On minute twenty-five of the roughly fifty-minute documentary, we can hear the song in which it is recommended that George W. Bush, Americans, and members of the Venezuelan opposition get sticks up their asses. The subtitles are mistaken when, in an effort to sugarcoat the lyrics, they translate the song into English by saying "a flogging, a stick for that ass." The video is available online at: http://www.youtube.com/watch?v=o2RQWpgEjBQ.

[22] Bart Jones, *¡Hugo! The Hugo Chávez Story,* p. 88.

[23] Ibid., p. 180.

[24] Ibid., p. 88.

[25] Charles Hardy, *Cowboy in Caracas.*

[26] Bart Jones, *¡Hugo! The Hugo Chávez Story,* p. 88.

[27] See Agustín Blanco Muñoz, *Habla Herma Marskman,* p. 73.

[28] Richard Gott, *In the Shadow of the Liberator,* p. 226. Chávez, incidentally, never attained the rank of colonel.

[29] Ibid., p. 227.

[30] The full pamphlet is contained in the "Materials Disseminated: September 1, 2006–February 28, 2007," itself part of the "Supplemental Statement, pursuant to Section 2 of the Foreign Agents Registration Act of 1938, as amended," which is required of all lobbyists for foreign governments, and which is available here: http://www.fara.gov/docs/5609-Supplemental-Statement-20070323-4.pdf.

[31] See e.g., http://www.washingtonpost.com/wp-dyn/content/article/2008/04/08/AR2008040803275_pf.html. See also the investigation carried out by Spain's prestigious *El País,* available here: http://www.elpais.com/articulo/portada/Bienvenidos/Chavezlandia/elpepusoceps/20061203elpepspor_6/Tes?print=1; or the report by NPR, available here: http://www.npr.org/templates/story/story.php?storyId=16727303.

[32] Hugo Chávez, "Aló Presidente 277," television broadcast, transcription available here: http://www.alopresidente.gob.ve/transcripciones/. See the references in the first note to this chapter.

[33] See the interview with Adán Chávez in *El Universal,* April 15, 2008, available here: http://www.eluniversal.com/2008/04/15/pol_art_el-deterioro-del-li_811363.shtml.

34 Hugo Chávez, "Aló Presidente 277"; see also: http://www.mci.gov.ve/pagina/28/7907/completa.html.

35 See: http://www.rnv.gov.ve/noticias/?act=ST&f=20&t=39411. The Chávez-Isturiz duo bears similarities to Laurel and Hardy or Abbot and Costello. On another occasion, Isturiz accused Chávez of "having smoked an egg-roll," i.e., an immense marijuana joint.

36 As far back as 1998, when Chávez was running for the Venezuelan presidency, Luis Castro Leiva wrote several op-ed pieces lamenting (and mocking) Chávez's forays into philology. One of the most famous of these pieces was called "La Vigorencia," after Chávez's invented word. See Luis Castro Leiva, *Los Espejos de la Conciencia: Escritos Periodísticos 1989–1999* (Caracas: El Centauro, 2001).

37 Matthew 19:24.

38 See: http://www.youtube.com/watch?v=8z1vtCxhT1M.

39 United Nations, *Human Development Report 1999* (New York: Oxford University Press, 1999), p. 134; United Nations, *Human Development Report 2007–2008* (New York: United Nations Development Programme, 2007), p. 230. Both reports are available online at http://hdr.undp.org/en/reports/global/hdr1999/.

40 See: http://www.youtube.com/watch?v=_Uq9F_WOKCU.

41 See http://www.youtube.com/watch?v=cajToqq3f_0.

42 When he was in the military academy, Chávez served as emcee in many a beauty pageant. A photo from one of these occasions appears in Cristina Marcano and Alberto Barrera Tyszka, *Hugo Chávez: The Definitive Biography*, photo insert after p. 170.

43 Camilo Chaparro, "*El que me acuse de dictador es un ignorante,*" pp. 70ff.

44 One crime that is particularly out of control in Venezuela is kidnapping. Jonathan Jakubowicz, a Venezuelan film director, made a brutal film based on the situation, called *Secuestro Express* ("Express Kidnapping"), which was widely distributed in the United States. Chávez's government claimed that the movie distorted the reality in Venezuela and accused Jakubowicz of being a traitor.

45 Available online here: http://www.derechos.org.ve/publicaciones/infanual/2005_06/index.html. Other studies confirm PROVEA's numbers, for example the study commissioned by the mayor of Chacao (a

municipality in Caracas). It is available here: http://www.chacao.gov.ve/plan180/anodespues.pdf.

[46] As this book was being edited, PROVEA's Annual Report for 2006–2007 came out. It is available here: http://www.derechos.org.ve/publicaciones/infanual/2006_07/index.html. The number of murders from January to September 2007 was 17,491, higher than the average of the last five years.

[47] See the official statistics by the U.S. Department of Defense here: http://www.defenselink.mil/news/casualty.pdf.

[48] See data from INCOSEC at: http://www.incosec.org/Microsoft%20 PowerPoint%20-%20plan180%20actualizado.pdf.

[49] See, e.g., the UN's own list on their *Human Development Report 2007– 2008*, pp. 322–25, available here: http://hdr.undp.org/en/reports/global/hdr2007-2008/. In the UN's current ranking, Venezuela appears in the fifth place worldwide. We should heed the UN's own admission: "Because of differences in the legal definition of offences, data are not strictly comparable across countries." Ibid., p. 325. We know what these definitional acrobatics mean in Venezuela.

[50] See, e.g., http://www.youtube.com/watch?v=oAST3RzPNIQ.

[51] See the report from Norwegian television here: http://www.youtube.com/watch?v=QIbmNfRNYKA; or the informative documentary by the BBC, here: http://www.veoh.com/videos/v15268013jCgWaK3?rank=9&.

[52] See Kim R. Holmes, Edwin J. Feulner, and Mary Anastasia O'Grady, *2008 Index of Economic Freedom* (Washington: The Heritage Foundation and Dow Jones & Company Inc., 2008), available online here: http://www.heritage.org/research/features/index/chapters/pdf/index2008 _execsum.pdf. The countries below Venezuela are, in descending order, Bangladesh, Belarus, Iran, Turkmenistan, Burma, Libya, Zimbabwe, Cuba, and North Korea. Coincidentally, some of these nations have become Venezuela's strongest allies.

[53] See: http://www.heritage.org/research/features/index/search.cfm.

[54] See: http://www.transparency.org/policy_research/surveys_indices/cpi/2007. The countries below Venezuela are, in descending order:

Congo, Equatorial Guinea, Guinea, Laos, Afghanistan, Chad, Sudan, Tonga, Uzbekistan, Haiti, Iraq, Myanmar, and Somalia.

55 See data at: http://www.transparency.org/policy_research/surveys_indices/cpi/previous_cpi__1/1999.

56 See, e.g., http://www.elmundo.es/elmundo/2008/07/14/internacional/1216054112.html.

57 See: www.francisteran.com. For more on Francis Terán's fate (and that of other former members of Chávez's government), see: http://broward.el-venezolano.net/articulo.asp?id=4229&edition=164.

58 Richard Gott, *Hugo Chávez and the Bolivarian Revolution* (London: Verso, 2000), p. 36.

59 See, e.g., Hugo Chávez Frías, *Habla el Comandante,* p. 58.

60 John Lynch, *Simón Bolívar: A Life* (New Haven: Yale University Press, 2006), p. 26.

61 Ibid., p. 307, n. 13.

62 Hugo Chávez Frías, *Habla el Comandante,* p. 125ff.

63 Cristina Marcano and Alberto Barrera Tyszka, *Hugo Chávez: The Definitive Biography of Venezuela's Controversial President* (New York: Random House, 2004), p. 5.

64 See, e.g., http://www.handsoffvenezuela.org/anniversary_caracazo_london.htm, in which we are told that "[i]t is now recognised that at least 3,000 people were killed, though some put the figure as high as 10,000." In keeping with the usual style of pro-Chávez literature, we are not given a single source to support such exorbitant figures.

65 The court's decision is available here: http://www1.umn.edu/humanrts/iachr/C/58-ing.html.

66 Charles Hardy, *Cowboy in Caracas,* p. 35; for his account of what happened, see p. 26ff.

67 Richard Gott, *Hugo Chávez and the Bolivarian Revolution,* p. 43.

68 The last title is taken from Angela Zago, *La Rebelion de los Angeles* (Caracas: Fuentes Editores, 1992), which was a homespun apology for Chávez. Zago later turned against Chávez, whom she now accuses of being a dictator, just as most of her partners in the early conspiracies have done.

69 Hugo Chávez Frías, *Habla el Comandante,* pp. 122–23.

70 Ibid., p. 150ff.

71 See: http://www.aporrea.org/actualidad/n69232.html.

72 See, e.g., http://www.fpolar.org.ve/nosotros/educacional/insurr/ 4febr92.html. This is the online update to the *Diccionario de Historia de Venezuela*.

73 Portions of the video are available here: http://www.youtube.com/ watch?v=NeT1ahL_PGY.

74 See, e.g., http://www.elpais.com/articulo/internacional/FUJIMORI/ _ALBERTO/ VENEZUELA/PERu/Peru/concede/asilo/politico/mil- itares/golpistas/ huyeron/Venezuela/elpepiint/19921201elpepiint_16/Tes/.

75 See, for example: http://www.aporrea.org/actualidad/n105417.html.

76 See, e.g., http://www.youtube.com/watch?v=VBUo-pYeVfQ.

77 See Juan José Caldera's effort to defend his father in Rafael Caldera, *De Carabobo a Puntofijo: Los Causahabientes* (Caracas: Libros Marcados, 2008), p. 162ff.

78 One example among many of that public sympathy for Chávez comes from José Ignacio Cabrujas, one of Venezuela's most important play- wrights and a noted intellectual. While he has effectively criticized the per- nicious Chávez mythology and opposes violence, he nonetheless joined in the choir of voices pleading for Chávez's release. See, e.g., José Ignacio Cabrujas, *El País según Cabrujas* (Caracas: Monteavila/El Diario de Caracas, 1992), pp. 210–12. Even Teodoro Petkoff, one of Venezuela's most judi- cious politicians and one of Chávez fiercest critics, admits that he would have voted for Chávez in 1998 had he not been certain that Chávez would win: See Teodoro Petkoff, *Una Segunda Opinión: La Venezuela de Chávez* (Caracas: Grijalbo Mondadori, 2000), p. 81.

79 Cristina Marcano and Alberto Barrera Tyszka, *Hugo Chávez: The Definitive Biography*, p. 110.

80 Andrés Oppenheimer, *Cuentos Chinos: El engaño de Washington, la mentira populista y la esperanza de América Latina* (Caracas: Random House Mon- dadori, 2005), p. 233.

81 Hugo Chávez Frías, *Habla el Comandante*, p. 177.

82 Ibid., p. 287.

83 Ibid., p. 425.

84 Ibid., pp. 548–49.

[85] The figures for Venezuelan elections are available on the website of Venezuela's Electoral Council, here: http://www.cne.gov.ve/estadisticas.php.

[86] Cristina Marcano and Alberto Barrera Tyszka, *Hugo Chávez: The Definitive Biography*, p. 151.

[87] Ibid.

[88] See, e.g., http://news.bbc.co.uk/hi/spanish/latin_america/newsid_1327000/1327544.stm.

[89] Cristina Marcano and Alberto Barrera Tyszka, *Hugo Chávez: The Definitive Biography*, p. 159.

[90] Ibid.

[91] Ibid., p. 156.

[92] See, e.g., http://www.youtube.com/watch?v=bhUBvf_oiPU.

[93] See, e.g., http://www.youtube.com/watch?v=sTPmm0LMfZg.

[94] See, e.g., http://www.youtube.com/watch?v=M3GWBcthgh8.

[95] See, e.g., http://www.cne.gob.ve/estadisticas/c010.pdf.

[96] See, e.g., http://www.constitucion.ve/03_const_presidente_docs7.html.

[97] See, e.g., http://www.youtube.com/watch?v=emsfxsTLCzk.

[98] See his speech here: http://www.youtube.com/watch?v=TSCdTKqVkbY

[99] See: República Bolivariana de Venezuela, Ley de la Fuerza Armada Bolivariana, *Gaceta Oficial Extraordinaria* 5891, July 31, 2008, available here: http://www.tsj.gov.ve/gaceta/gacetaoficial.asp.

[100] See: República Bolivariana de Venezuela, Ley de Turismo, "Exposición de Motivos," *Gaceta Oficial Extraordinaria* 5889, July 31, 2008, available here: http://www.tsj.gov.ve/gaceta/gacetaoficial.asp.

[101] See: República Bolivariana de Venezuela, Ley de Defensa de las Personas en el Acceso a Bienes y Servicios, Article 139, *Gaceta Oficial Extraordinaria* 5889, July 31, 2008, available here: http://www.tsj.gov.ve/gaceta/gacetaoficial.asp.

[102] Ibid., Article 143.

[103] See, for example, República Bolivariana de Venezuela, Ley de Transporte Ferroviario, Article 89, *Gaceta Oficial Extraordinaria* 5889, July 31, 2008, available here: http://www.tsj.gov.ve/gaceta/gacetaoficial.asp.

[104] See Miquilena's press conference here: http://www.youtube.com/watch?v=cqxai05ZNoc;

http://www.youtube.com/watch?v=L0UbBGidkQs;
http://www.youtube.com/watch?v=S65U_fQM9So; and
http://www.youtube.com/watch?v=83azOt3wlHQ.

[105] Regarding the regional elections of November 2008, Chávez has threatened "war" if the opposition were to win a few governorships:
http://www.youtube.com/watch?v=B6zh_kmdjhU. This sort of intimidating discourse is absolutely normal in Venezuela nowadays.

[106] See, e.g., http://buscador.eluniversal.com/2008/06/16/pol_ava_russian:-
inhabilitac_16A1684561.shtml. For the official list of candidates who were
administratively (without a conviction, and without the right to defend
themselves) declared ineligible to run for office, see here:
http://www.cgr.gov.ve/smc/pdf/Sanciones/INH_SANC.pdf.

[107] See, e.g., http://www.lacea.org/HAND%20OUT%20LACEA%20
ELECCIONES/2007/CVs%202007/Ricardo%20Hausmann%20CV.pdf;
and http://ksghome.harvard.edu/~rhausma/new/carterresponse.pdf. An
additional study, published in *International Statistical Review,* the flagship
peer-reviewed journal of the International Statistical Institute, also suggests
a great likelihood of fraud; the study is available online here:
http://isi.cbs.nl/ISR/ISR74-3.htm.

[108] See: http://www.youtube.com/watch?v=4UY1AfFMN2I.

[109] See: http://www.youtube.com/watch?v=7GDQ8NwoHVc.

[110] For soccer announcing, see, e.g., http://www.youtube.com/
watch?v=Q0y3BiuTX7Y.

[111] See: http://www.periodismoenlinea.org/200809122103/Desde-Peru/
Venezuela-acusa-a-Bayly-ante-la-OEA-por-intentar-asesinar-a-Hugo-
Chavez.html.

[112] The law passed in May 2008, Ley del Sistema Nacional de Inteligencia y
Contrainteligencia (Law of the National System of Intelligence and
Counter-Intelligence), gives Chávez many more powers, establishing, now
under the color of law, a repressive police state. See some of the reactions
by human rights groups: http://www.eluniversal.com/2008/05/31/
pol_art_ley-de-inteligencia_885751.shtml.

[113] See: http://www.youtube.com/watch?v=IBmJgzkbuwM.

[114] In the annual report for 2005–2006 published by PROVEA, Venezuela's
most important human rights organization, we find copies of memoranda

in which members of Chávez's government threaten employees if they do not attend Chávez's events. The reports are available here: http://www.derechos.org.ve/publicaciones/infanual/2005_06/index.html.

[115] See, e.g., http://www.telegraph.co.uk/news/worldnews/1581212/Phone-led-US-experts-to-Farc-leader-Raul-Reyes.html.

Chapter Three: Chavez's Impact on Venezuela and Beyond

[1] See: http://www.youtube.com/watch?v=jS_4TLvphW8.

[2] See Aleida Guevara, *Hugo Chavez and the New Latin America: An Interview with Hugo Chávez* (New York: Ocean Press, 2005), p. 15; or see the "documentary" by the same name and producer issued on DVD.

[3] Among many other instances, Chávez proudly uses the expression in the documentary with Aleida, just referenced.

[4] Translating from the Carib language is not easy. The official Office of the Vice President provides the translation I am using, a translation also endorsed by a famous Chávez supporter, Roberto Hernandez Montoya, here: http://www.vicepresidencia.gov.ve/web/index.php?option=com_content&task=view&id=1453&Itemid=2; and http://www.analitica.com/bitblio/roberto/america.asp. One of Venezuela's foremost living historians, Guillermo Morón, also agrees with this translation: http://www.2001.com.ve/articulo_opinion.asp?registro=2527.

[5] With Venezuelan taxpayers' money, for example, a new political support group for Chávez has been created, with the name "Ana Karina Rote" (see http://www.aporrea.org/actualidad/n15599.html; and http://www.aporrea.org/actualidad/n12454.html). Fittingly, given the spirit of the Carib motto, this Chavista organization has already engaged (in conjunction with the Ministry of Science and Technology) in anti-Semitic activities, as reported by the Coordinating Forum for Countering Antisemitism, here: http://www.antisemitism.org.il/eng/search/?page=1&country=65. Interestingly, the Forum does not say a word about the meaning of the organization's name.

[6] Even the opposition uses the term for itself: See www.redescualidos.net. See also the government-sponsored www.antiescualidos.com.

[7] See Chávez reacting to a (perfectly sensible) question that he does not like, here: http://www.veoh.com/videos/v15268013jCgWaK3?rank=9&.

[8] See: http://www.youtube.com/watch?v=2LuOQjhg8BU.

[9] See: http://europa.eu/bulletin/en/200407/p105024.htm. For more on the referendum, see: http://www.voanews.com/uspolicy/archive/2004-08/a-2004-08-30-10-1.cfm.

[10] See the documentary on the referendum and the lists that Chávez's regime created, here: http://www.youtube.com/watch?v=2LuOQjhg8BU. A version with English subtitles is available here: http://www.urru.org/DDHH_Index.htm. (Click on the sixth link in the column titled "Videos y Grabaciones.") If such results followed from merely voting in a referendum, the reader may now understand my reasons for using a pseudonym: what would Chávez or his hordes seek to do to the author of a book like this—or to the author's relatives?

[11] See: http://www.youtube.com/watch?v=kLf08O3D_f0.

[12] See: http://www.youtube.com/watch?v=binMjEiS8AY.

[13] See: http://www.youtube.com/watch?v=Yw7yAbTQ5IM.

[14] See: http://www.youtube.com/watch?v=izM_JwEkWPs.

[15] See: http://www.youtube.com/watch?v=CwmeEPsqILI. The theme of "working for free" is a favorite of Chávez, as this other incident shows: http://www.youtube.com/watch?v=nNFsa4KIgfE.

[16] See Chávez's performance here: http://www.youtube.com/watch?v=9fgAdq_SLYU.

[17] http://www.leyresorte.gob.ve/index.asp.

[18] Since Chávez seized power, it has become very hard to translate Venezuelan figures into internationally understandable terms. For example, there is an official exchange rate, according to which one United States dollar is equivalent to 2,150 bolivars. But since February 2003, Chávez has prohibited the free exchange of currency. On the one hand, this prohibition has given rise to a huge black market—though Chávez promised, in vain, that there would never be a black market. The exchange rate fluctuates widely, but it has been as high as three times the official rate. On the other hand, the exchange controls have generated a fabulous source of corruption, since Chávez's friends, as one would expect, have an easier time obtaining foreign currency at the unrealistically low official rate.

[19] See Reporters Without Borders, *International Community Urged to Rally to Defence of Venezuela's Media after RCTV's Closure*, available at

www.rsf.org/article.php3?id_article+22326, last visited on June 2008. See also their *Annual Report 2008* on Venezuela, available at http://www.rsf.org/article.php3?id_article=25598. For more on Chávez's abuse against freedom of the press and on his persecution of journalists, see the reports and communiqués from the Inter American Press Association here: http://mercury.websitewelcome.com/~sipiapa/resolucion.php?id=281&tipo=3&idioma=sp&asamblea=5; http://mercury.websitewelcome.com/~sipiapa/informe.php?id=300&idioma=sp&asamblea=5. More here: http://www.globovision.com/news.php?nid=96578; and here: http://news.bbc.co.uk/2/hi/americas/3524760.stm

20 See the reports listed in the previous note.

21 See: http://www.youtube.com/watch?v=Wd4E-Af82Uc.

22 Stephen Holden, "Tumult in Venezuela's Presidential Palace, Seen Up Close," *New York Times,* November 5, 2003.

23 See: http://www.11abril.com/index/especiales/chavezthefilm.

24 See: http://rogerebert.suntimes.com/apps/pbcs.dll/article?AID=/20031031/REVIEWS/310310305/1023.

25 Ibid.

26 See: http://video.google.com/videosearch?q=radiografia+de+una+mentira#.

27 See: http://www.guardian.co.uk/news/2007/may/26/leadersandreply.mainsection6.

28 See: http://www.forbes.com/lists/2006/10/Rank_5.html.

29 See: http://www.rnv.gov.ve/noticias/index.php?act=ST&f=2&t=5988.

30 See: http://news.bbc.co.uk/hi/spanish/latin_america/newsid_3822000/3822765.stm.

31 See, for example, the account in the *Annual Report 2008 for Venezuela,* published by Reporters Without Borders, available here: http://www.rsf.org/article.php3?id_article=25598.

32 See: http://www.usdoj.gov/criminal/fara/links/search.html. Some of Chávez's other fans, like Gregory Wilpert, Charles Hardy, and Bart Jones, among many others, including professors and congressmen, are in contact with the lobbyists paid by the Venezuelan government.

33 Eva Golinger, *The Chávez Code: Cracking U.S. Intervention in Venezuela* (Northampton, Mass.: Olive Branch Press, 2006). For more on Golinger

and her other book, *Bush versus Chávez* (of a similar tenor), and her pro-Chávez crusade, visit her website: http://www. chavezcode.com/.

[34] For this particular example, see Eva Golinger, *The Chávez Code*, p. 202; but more generally look through the ineffectual set of documents on pp. 134–202.

[35] See: http://www.eluniversal.com/2008/05/31/til_art_no-llegan-libros-al_885791.shtml. A recent op-ed piece in Spain's prestigious newspaper *El País* describes how Chávez has made the importing of books extremely difficult, and has simultaneously flooded Venezuelan libraries with his own favored books. See: http://www.elpais.com/articulo/opinion/Caudillo/Chavez/elpepiopi/20090516elpepiopi_2/Tes. In recent months, there has been a marked increase in reports of book burnings by the Chávez regime. See: http://www.eluniversal.com/2009/03/24/opi_art_quema-de-libros_1309302.shtml; and http://www.eluniversal.com/2009/04/01/til_art_auditan-35-bibliotec_1330113.shtml.

[36] See: http://www.youtube.com/watch?v=EpamEiuzAVo.

[37] The subtitles in Spanish correctly rendered Chomsky's words as condemned to "life in prison."

[38] See: http://www.youtube.com/watch?v=x_bTj227nqw. This is the version of the interview as it was broadcast in Venezuela, and as it is available online. Judging by some of the other transcriptions found on the Web (say, here: http://www.ludd.net/retort/msg00920.html), the actual interview differs somewhat, though not significantly, from the edited broadcast version.

[39] See their reaction to the savage manner in which they were kicked out from Venezuela here: http://www.nybooks.com/articles/22033.

[40] See, e.g., http://redpepper.blogs.com/venezuela/2006/02/by_providing_su.html.

[41] The interview was conducted by Kabir Joshi-Vijayan and Matthew Skogstad-Stubbs. See http://www.venezuelanalysis.com/analysis/2389.

[42] See: http://www.globovision.com/news.php?nid=94916; and http://www.youtube.com/watch?v=cqxai05ZNoc.

[43] See, e.g., their main report, "The Chávez Regime: Fostering Anti-Semitism and Supporting Radical Islam," available here: http://www.adl.org/main_International_Affairs/venezuela_anti_semitism_report.htm. Follow

the links therein for more such reports. Against the background of Chávez's anti-Semitism, it is not surprising that he has invited Norman Finkelstein, Chomsky's pseudo-academic underling, to visit and lecture in Venezuela. See, e.g., http://www.rebelion.org/noticia.php?id=56923; and http://www.commentarymagazine.com/viewarticle.cfm/hugo-ch-vez-s-jewish-problem-11455.

44 See: http://www.philosophicalgourmet.com/.

45 See: http://leiterreports.typepad.com/blog/2007/02/has_hugh_Chávez.html.

46 Here: http://www.venezuelanalysis.com/.

47 See: http://leiterreports.typepad.com/blog/2007/02/has_hugh_Chávez.html.

48 See: http://www.youtube.com/watch?v=AZa3Slwgup0. This video includes, also, a clip of an undignified Supreme Court, in session, singing and dancing to the tune of "Uh, Ah, Chávez no se va" ("Chávez is not leaving").

49 See, e.g., http://leiterreports.typepad.com/blog/2007/02/has_hugh_Chávez.html. The link to Wilpert's article is broken, but it can be found here: http://www.venezuelanalysis.com/analysis?page=118.

50 See the relevant piece of legislation: http://frwebgate.access.gpo.gov/cgi bin/getdoc.cgi?dbname=107_cong_public_laws&docid=f:publ210.107.

51 See: http://www.analitica.com/BITBLIO/anc/constitucion1999.asp.

52 See him embracing and praising Chávez here: http://www.youtube.com/watch?v=SFT8Vyvwqf4. (In the audience you can see Cornel West.) For the support of Glover's movies, see: http://www.time.com/time/world/article/0,8599,1624992,00.html?xid=feed-cnn-topics.

53 See: http://www.timesonline.co.uk/tol/news/world/us_and_americas/article2801025.ece.

54 Charles Hardy, *Cowboy in Caracas: A North American's Memoir of Venezuela's Democratic Revolution* (Willimantic, Conn.: Curbstone Press, 2007), back cover.

55 Bart Jones, *¡Hugo! The Hugo Chávez Story from Mud Hut to Perpetual Revolution* (Hanover, N.H.: Steerforth Press, 2007). Jones is perhaps a bit less strident than Hardy.

56 Read the report of part of the visit and the "interview" of Bourgeois that Hardy did, here: http://www.venezuelanalysis.com/analysis/321; and

watch Bourgeois's excitement as he shakes hands with Chávez here: http://rodriguez.mikel.googlepages.com/soaworkshop.

[57] See: http://www.khaleejtimes.com/DisplayArticleNew. asp?xfile=data/middleeast/2006/September/middleeast_ September479.xml&section=middleeast; and http://www.isj.org.uk/index.php4?id=243&issue=112.

[58] See Sean Penn rave about Chávez (parroting some of Chomsky's flawed views) here: http://www.youtube.com/watch?v=xh2Lm_F58Nc. For a more protracted version of Penn's support of Chávez, see here: http://www.thenation.com/doc/20081215/penn/single.

[59] In *The New Yorker,* September 10, 2001, available here: http://www.newyorker.com/archive/2001/09/10/010910fa_fact_ anderson.

[60] *New York Review of Books,* October 6, 2005; and October 20, 2005.

[61] This sort of superficial treatment of books when they are not from an in-house author may explain the well-known nicknames *New York Review of (Each Other's) Books* and *New York Review (Formerly of Books).*

[62] See the official communiqué from the Venezuelan government in the midst of the crisis in Zimbabwe in December 2008, here: http://www.mre.gov.ve/Noticias/A2008/comunic-353.htm.

[63] The letter is available, in Spanish, here: http://www.analitica.com/ bitblioteca/hchavez/carta_chacal.asp.

[64] Chávez's affection for the Jackal has remained unabated over the years, as he regularly mentions him in very friendly terms. The last time was at the OPEC conference in Caracas on June 1, 2006, when Chávez referred to the convicted terrorist as his "good friend"—see, e.g., http://www. eluniversal.com/2006/06/01/pol_ava_01A715651.shtml.

[65] See, "La Familia de Carlos 'El Chacal' espera mas gestos de Chávez," *El Nuevo Herald,* April 19, 1999, p. 1B.

[66] See Chávez's recitation here: http://www.youtube.com/watch?v= d7iwfDycbFk.

[67] FARC is included in the United States government's official list of terrorist organizations: http://www.state.gov/s/ct/rls/fs/37191.htm.

[68] See: http://www.youtube.com/watch?v=zhikWglQ1us.

[69] See: http://www.youtube.com/watch?v=LYBLp_YHznc.

[70] See: http://www.youtube.com/watch?v=794QUee0YS8.

[71] See: http://www.youtube.com/watch?v=LF0Us1FeLWQ.

[72] See: http://www.youtube.com/watch?v=Cbvnx0y0crU.

[73] See: http://www.youtube.com/watch?v=RZTN91DaxII. ELN refers to the National Liberation Army.

[74] See: http://www.youtube.com/watch?v=i8LP5kZt4UA.

[75] See: http://www.youtube.com/watch?v=i8LP5kZt40A.

[76] See: http://www.mre.gob.ve/Noticias/A2008/comunic-227.htm.

[77] And yet, at least one of Chávez's fans has it exactly backwards. As he recalls the 1999 mudslides in Venezuela, Charles Hardy claims that "the opposition criticized the government for what had happened because the polls were allowed to be open later that day," when Venezuelans were voting on Chávez's new constitution. He satirizes this opposition by claiming that for them, "now the government was responsible for everything, even a tragedy of nature." But the opposition never blamed the government for the mudslides, only for downplaying the magnitude of the torrential rains that had been falling for weeks before the referendum. Instead of heeding the clamorous requests to delay the referendum in order to help those already made homeless, Chávez arrogantly quoted Bolívar's famous words on the occasion of the earthquake of 1812: "If nature opposes our plans, we will defeat it, and force it to obey us." Nature, of course, did not obey. Chávez's bravado cost thousands of Venezuelans their lives; as Hardy correctly acknowledges, some estimates speak of 100,000 deaths. See Charles Hardy, *Cowboy in Caracas*, p. 50.

[78] See: http://www.usatoday.com/life/people/2007-12-30-stone_N.htm. For more on the documentary itself, see: http://www.variety.com/VR1117997180.html.

[79] See: http://www.reuters.com/article/latestCrisis/idUSN0I612491.

[80] See: http://www.youtube.com/watch?v=XiCvAbE3AoA. It is hard to doubt Betancourt's honesty here: She is, after all, rather friendly with Chávez, and has expressed more gratitude to him than to Uribe, though Chávez had nothing to do with her release and Uribe everything to do with it.

[81] See: http://www.youtube.com/watch?v=zWdQxFIEYN4.

[82] See: http://www.rnv.gov.ve/noticias/index.php?act=ST&f=2&t=44467.

[83] See: http://www.volarenvenezuela.com/vev/modules.php?name= News&file=article&sid=1972.

[84] The quotation is taken from Greg Wilpert's pro-Chávez website, here: www.venezuelanalysis.com/analysis/1654. Wilpert believes that Iran is an excellent partner for Venezuela.

[85] See: http://news.bbc.co.uk/2/hi/americas/5354812.stm.

[86] See: http://www.usatoday.com/news/world/2007-01-14-iran-venezuela_x.htm.

[87] See: http://news.bbc.co.uk/2/hi/americas/5354812.stm.

[88] See: http://online.wsj.com/video/preventing-a-nuclear-chavez/2E88FC63-C753-40D1-8ADD-A91ABAEB744A.html; http://frontpagemagazine. com/Articles/Read.aspx?GUID=49678FEB-D267-43D9-BDF0-FBF-FCC82F68B; http://www.guardian.co.uk/world/2007/jun/29/ venezuela.lukeharding; and http://www.foxnews.com/story/ 0,2933,429441,00.html.

[89] See: http://news.bbc.co.uk/2/hi/middle_east/4680294.stm.

[90] See: http://www.washingtontimes.com/news/2006/mar/13/20060313-121547-4071r/; http://www.eluniversal.com/2008/06/19/pol_art_ acusan-a-diplomatico_911470.shtml; or this report by Michael Rubin for the American Enterprise Institute for Public Policy Research: http://www.aei.org/publications/pubID.27658/pub_detail.asp.

[91] See: http://www.lastampa.it/_web/cmstp/tmplRubriche/giornalisti/ grubrica.asp?ID_blog=43&ID_articolo=1106&ID_sezione=&sezione=.

[92] United States Congress, *Venezuela: Terrorism Hub of South America?* Hearing Before the Subcommittee on International Terrorism and Nonproliferation of the Committee on International Relations, House of Representatives, 109th Congress, 2nd Session, July 13, 2006 (Washington: U.S. Government Printing Office, 2006), p. 2. A transcript is available here: http://commdocs.house.gov/committees/intlrel/hfa28638.000/ hfa28638_0.htm.

[93] See: http://www.treas.gov/press/releases/hp1036.htm. See also the article in the *Washington Times* here: http://www.washingtontimes.com/news/ 2008/jul/07/us-ties-caracas-to-hezbollah-aid/?page=1.

[94] United States Congress, *Venezuela: Terrorism Hub,* p. 2.

[95] Ibid., p. 22.

[96] Ibid., p. 4.

[97] Ibid., p. 2.

[98] Ibid., pp. 16–17.

[99] See: http://news.bbc.co.uk/2/hi/americas/5082006.stm; and http://www.aporrea.org/tiburon/n90037.html.

[100] See: http://www.youtube.com/watch?v=MS6WBcIhgh8.

[101] See: http://www.eluniverso.com/2008/07/24/0001/14/9948292A78C2438BB919E18A539D7770.html.

[102] See: http://www.kommersant.com/p773951/arms_trade/; and http://www.youtube.com/watch?v=9h5sqOPmaUA.

[103] See: http://www.elimparcial.es:6681/hemeroteca/2008/07/23/contenido/19381.html.

[104] See: http://www.airforcetimes.com/news/2008/09/ap_russian_bombers_091008/.

[105] See: http://edition.cnn.com/2008/WORLD/americas/09/22/russia.venezuela.ap/index.html.

[106] Perhaps nowhere is this sort of blandness more apparent than in Jennifer L. McCoy's testimony to the United States Congress, found in *Venezuela: Looking Ahead*, Hearing Before the Subcommittee on the Western Hemisphere of the House Committee on Foreign Affairs, 110th Congress, 2nd Session, July 17, 2008 (Washington: U.S. Government Printing Office, 2008), pp. 45–53. Available here: http://foreignaffairs.house.gov/110/43520.pdf. It is not surprising that McCoy was the second-in-command (just below Jimmy Carter himself) for the Carter Center's mission overseeing the referendum of 2004, which I described above, and which caused most sensible Venezuelans to repudiate the Carter Center. Mere days after her report was submitted, several of her assertions were proven wrong– for instance, regarding Chavez's disqualification of opposition candidates, she tried to suggest that there were Chávez supporters among the disqualified.

[107] See, e.g., http://www.whitehouse.gov/news/releases/2008/08/20080818-1.html; and http://www.el-nacional.com/www/site/p_contenido.php?q=nodo/41026.

[108] See: http://www.reuters.com/article/GCA-Russia/idUSL2297503220080722; http://www.nydailynews.com/latino/

espanol/2008/07/23/2008-07-23_chvez_plantea_posible_base_
militar_rusa_.html; and http://www.tehrantimes.com/index_
View.asp?code=173789. Two days later, the Venezuelan government
denied the reports of a Russian base in Venezuela, because Chávez did
not use the word "base." True, Chávez did not use that word, but he did
say that he would welcome, with all honors and warmth, any military
presence in Venezuela, as was widely reported and can be seen in the
video here: http://www.youtube.com/watch?v=S1hvH9tJFCM.

[109] United States Congress, *Venezuela: Terrorism Hub*, p. 1.

[110] Ibid.

Appendix: The Chávez Lobby in the United States

[1] See, e.g., John J. Mearsheimer and Stephen M. Walt, *The Israel Lobby and U.S. Foreign Policy* (New York: Farrar, Straus & Giroux, 2007). James Petras, Paul Findley, Noam Chomsky, and others make appearances.

[2] See: http://portal.gobiernoenlinea.ve/cartelera/CirculosBolivarianos.html. Unless otherwise noted, all URLs in this appendix were functioning when last visited on May 11, 2009.

[3] See: http://www.vicuk.org/.

[4] See: http://www.venezuelasolidarity.org.uk/.

[5] See: http://www.venezuelasolidarity.org/.

[6] See: http://www.usdoj.gov/criminal/fara/.

[7] See: http://www.haitipolicy.org/content/2132.htm.

[8] See: http://www.fara.gov/docs/2165-Exhibit-AB-20031021-HPDS8L04.pdf.

[9] See: http://www.fara.gov/docs/2165-Exhibit-AB-20040804-I2184T04.pdf.

[10] See: http://www.fara.gov/docs/2165-Exhibit-AB-20031021-HPDS8L04.pdf.

[11] See: http://www.fara.gov/docs/1750-Exhibit-AB-20000425-H9QYAN02.pdf.

[12] See: http://www.fara.gov/docs/5452-Exhibit-AB-20010817-GRSDYV02.pdf.

[13] See: http://www.dutkoworldwide.com/what_we_do/.

[14] See: http://www.fara.gov/docs/5452-Exhibit-AB-20010817-GRSDYV02.pdf.

[15] See: http://www.fara.gov/docs/5564-Exhibit-AB-20030619-HI2WCM03.pdf; and http://www.fara.gov/docs/5564-Exhibit-AB-20031022-HPFLMG02.pdf.

[16] See: http://www.fara.gov/docs/5624-Exhibit-AB-20040520-HYN72M04.pdf.

[17] See: http://www.time.com/time/specials/packages/article/0,28804,1841778_1841779_1841804,00.html.

[18] See: http://www.luminastrategies.com/staff.shtml

[19] See: http://www.mica.edu/blackpanther/article.cfm?entry=80, last visited on December 20, 2008.

[20] See: http://www.fara.gov/docs/5764-Exhibit-AB-20060908-1.pdf.

[21] See: http://www.fara.gov/docs/5609-Amendment-20040302-IIVRFBN04.pdf.

[22] As we have seen throughout this book, many of Chávez's supporters claim that the United States government is engaged in a campaign of misinformation regarding Chávez's regime. See, for example, the books by Eva Golinger, Charles Hardy, and Gregory Wilpert, discussed earlier.

[23] For example, Mark H. Stumpf, the signatory to the contract between Chávez's government (duly represented by the Venezuelan embassy in the United States) and Arnold & Porter, also claims to have represented Chávez's government on the "Exchange Offer for US $4.4 Billion of outstanding bonds." See, e.g., http://aporter.com/professionals.cfm?action=view&id=116.

[24] See: http://www.fara.gov/docs/5452-Exhibit-AB-20010817-GRSDYV02.pdf.

[25] See: http://www.redlinkvenezuela.com/index.html. Incidentally, as of September 11, 2008, the VIO officially changed its name to "Latin America Information Office LLC"; see, e.g.: http://www.fara.gov/docs/5609-Exhibit-C-20080915-1.pdf.

[26] See: http://www.fara.gov/docs/5609-Supplemental-Statement-20040829-I5KUBS02.pdf.

[27] See: http://www.fara.gov/docs/5609-Supplemental-Statement-20050228-IEH7IP04.pdf.

[28] See: http://www.fara.gov/docs/5609-Supplemental-Statement-20050930-1.pdf.

[29] See: http://www.fara.gov/docs/5609-Supplemental-Statement-20060328-2.pdf.

[30] See: http://www.fara.gov/docs/5609-Supplemental-Statement-20060929-3.pdf.

[31] See: http://www.fara.gov/docs/5609-Supplemental-Statement-20070323-4.pdf.

[32] See: http://www.fara.gov/docs/5609-Supplemental-Statement-20070920-5.pdf.

[33] See: http://www.fara.gov/docs/5609-Supplemental-Statement-20080327-6.pdf.

[34] See: http://www.fara.gov/docs/5609-Supplemental-Statement-20080923-7.pdf.

[35] See: http://www.manta.com/coms2/dnbcompany_c73qnf.

[36] See: http://www.fara.gov/docs/5609-Supplemental-Statement-20050930-1.pdf.

[37] See: http://www.fara.gov/docs/5609-Supplemental-Statement-20060328-2.pdf.

[38] See: http://www.fara.gov/docs/5609-Supplemental-Statement-20060929-3.pdf.

[39] See: http://www.fara.gov/docs/5609-Supplemental-Statement-20070323-4.pdf.

[40] See: http://www.fara.gov/docs/5609-Supplemental-Statement-20070920-5.pdf.

[41] See: http://www.fara.gov/docs/5609-Supplemental-Statement-20050228-IEH7IP04.pdf.

[42] See: http://www.washingtonpost.com/wp-dyn/content/discussion/2008/11/20/DI2008112002452.html.

[43] See: http://www.cepr.net/.

[44] See: http://www.fara.gov/docs/5609-Supplemental-Statement-20040829-I5KUBS02.pdf; http://www.fara.gov/docs/5609-Supplemental-Statement-20050228-IEH7IP04.pdf; http://www.fara.gov/docs/5609-Supplemental-Statement-20050930-1.pdf; http://www.fara.gov/docs/5609-Supplemental-Statement-20060328-2.pdf;

http://www.fara.gov/docs/5609-Supplemental-Statement-20060929-
3.pdf; http://www.fara.gov/docs/5609-Supplemental-Statement-
20070323-4.pdf; http://www.fara.gov/docs/5609-Supplemental-
Statement-20070920-5.pdf; http://www.fara.gov/docs/5609-
Supplemental-Statement-20080327-6.pdf; and http://www.fara.gov/
docs/5609-Supplemental-Statement-20080923-7.pdf.

45 Mark Weisbrot is extremely active in his support of Chávez, as we have
seen. Laura Safer Espinoza, too, has written about Chávez and has visited
Venezuela in order to report (glowingly) on his regime: see, e.g.,
http://www.nlginternational.org/news/article.php?nid=31; and
http://milwaukee.indymedia.org/en/2007/04/207148.shtml.

46 See: http://www.fara.gov/docs/5609-Supplemental-Statement-
20040829-I5KUBS02.pdf; http://www.fara.gov/docs/5609-
Supplemental-Statement-20050228-IEH7IP04.pdf; http://www.fara.gov/
docs/ 5609 Supplemental-Statement-20050930-1.pdf; http://www.fara.
gov/ docs/5609-Supplemental-Statement-20060328-2.pdf; http://www.
fara. gov/docs/5609-Supplemental-Statement-20060929-3.pdf;
http://www.fara.gov/docs/5609-Supplemental-Statement-20070323-
4.pdf; http://www.fara.gov/docs/5609-Supplemental-Statement
20070920-5.pdf; http://www.fara.gov/docs/5609 Supplemental-
Statement-20080327-6.pdf; and http://www.fara.gov/docs/5609-
Supplemental-Statement-20080923 7.pdf.

47 See: http://www.nuamerica.org/Filmmakers.html.

48 The March 10, 2006, contact via email is listed on the report for the six-
month period ending February 28, 2006, and also on the report for the
six-month period ending August 31, 2006. The second report does not
include the words "at cost." Both misspell Wager's name as "Wagger." See:
http://www.fara.gov/docs/5609-Supplemental-Statement 20040829-
I5KUBS02.pdf; http://www.fara.gov/docs/5609 Supplemental-Statement-
20050228-IEH7IP04.pdf; http://www.fara.gov/docs/5609-
Supplemental-Statement-20050930-1.pdf; http://www.fara.gov/
docs/5609-Supplemental-Statement-20060328-2.pdf; http://www.fara.
gov/docs/5609-Supplemental-Statement-20060929-3.pdf;
http://www.fara.gov/docs/5609-Supplemental-Statement-20070323-
4.pdf; http://www.fara.gov/docs/5609-Supplemental-Statement-

20070920-5.pdf; http://www.fara.gov/docs/5609-Supplemental-Statement-20080327-6.pdf; and http://www.fara.gov/docs/5609-Supplemental-Statement-20080923-7.pdf.

[49] See: http://www.fara.gov/docs/5609-Supplemental-Statement-20040829-I5KUBS02.pdf; http://www.fara.gov/docs/5609-Supplemental-Statement-20050228-IEH7IP04.pdf; http://www.fara.gov/docs/5609-Supplemental-Statement-20050930-1.pdf; http://www.fara.gov/docs/5609-Supplemental-Statement-20060328-2.pdf; http://www.fara.gov/docs/5609-Supplemental-Statement-20060929-3.pdf; http://www.fara.gov/docs/5609-Supplemental-Statement-20070323-4.pdf; http://www.fara.gov/docs/5609-Supplemental- Statement-20070920-5.pdf; http://www.fara.gov/docs/5609-Supplemental-Statement-20080327-6.pdf; and http://www.fara.gov/docs/5609-Supplemental-Statement-20080923-7.pdf.

[50] See: http://www.fara.gov/docs/5609-Supplemental-Statement-20040829-I5KUBS02.pdf; http://www.fara.gov/docs/5609-Supplemental-Statement-20050228-IEH7IP04.pdf; http://www.fara.gov/docs/5609-Supplemental-Statement-20050930-1.pdf; http://www.fara.gov/ docs/5609-Supplemental-Statement-20060328-2.pdf; http://www.fara.gov/docs/5609-Supplemental-Statement-20060929-3.pdf; http://www.fara.gov/docs/5609-Supplemental-Statement-20070323-4.pdf; http://www.fara.gov/docs/5609-Supplemental-Statement-20070920-5.pdf; http://www.fara.gov/docs/5609-Supplemental-Statement-20080327-6.pdf; and http://www.fara.gov/docs/5609-Supplemental-Statement-20080923-7.pdf.

[51] The press release is available online here: http://serrano.house.gov/PressRelease.aspx?NewsID=1116, last visited December 20, 2008. On May 11, 2009, the text was found here: http://serrano.house.gov/NewsDetail. aspx?ID=72.

[52] See: http://www.fara.gov/docs/5609-Supplemental-Statement-20040829-I5KUBS02.pdf; http://www.fara.gov/docs/5609-Supplemental-Statement-20050228-IEH7IP04.pdf; http://www.fara.gov/docs/5609-Supplemental-Statement-20050930-1.pdf; http://www.fara.gov/docs/5609-Supplemental-Statement-20060328-2.pdf; http://www.fara.gov/docs/5609-Supplemental-Statement-20060929-3.pdf;

http://www.fara.gov/docs/5609-Supplemental-Statement-20070323-
4.pdf; http://www.fara.gov/docs/5609-Supplemental-Statement-
20070920-5.pdf; http://www.fara.gov/docs/5609-Supplemental-
Statement-20080327-6.pdf; and http://www.fara.gov/docs/5609-
Supplemental-Statement-20080923-7.pdf.

53 See: http://www.fara.gov/docs/5609-Supplemental-Statement-
20040829-I5KUBS02.pdf; http://www.fara.gov/docs/5609-
Supplemental-Statement-20050228-IEH7IP04.pdf; http://www.fara.gov/
docs/5609-Supplemental-Statement-20050930-1.pdf; http://www.fara.
gov/docs/5609 Supplemental-Statement-20060328-2.pdf; http://www.
fara.gov/docs/5609-Supplemental-Statement-20060929-3.pdf;
http://www.fara. gov/docs/5609-Supplemental-Statement-20070323-
4.pdf; http://www.fara.gov/docs/5609-Supplemental-Statement-
20070920-5.pdf; http://www.fara.gov/docs/5609-Supplemental-
Statement-20080327-6.pdf; and http://www.fara.gov/docs/5609-
Supplemental- Statement-20080923-7.pdf.

54 See: http://www.fara.gov/docs/5609-Supplemental-Statement-
20040829-I5KUBS02.pdf; http://www.fara.gov/docs/5609-
Supplemental-Statement-20050228-IEH7IP04.pdf; http://www.fara.gov/
docs/5609-Supplemental-Statement-20050930-1.pdf;
http://www.fara.gov/docs/5609-Supplemental-Statement-20060328-2.
pdf; http://www.fara.gov/docs/5609-Supplemental-Statement-
20060929-3.pdf; http://www.fara.gov/docs/5609-Supplemental-
Statement-20070323-4.pdf; http://www.fara.gov/docs/5609-
Supplemental-Statement-20070920 5.pdf; http://www.fara.gov/docs/
5609-Supplemental Statement-20080327-6.pdf; and http://www.fara.
gov/docs/5609-Supplemental-Statement-20080923-7.pdf.

55 See: http://www.fara.gov/docs/5609-Supplemental Statement-
20040829-I5KUBS02.pdf; http://www.fara.gov/docs/5609-
Supplemental-Statement-20050228-IEH7IP04.pdf; http://www.fara.gov/
docs/5609-Supplemental-Statement-20050930-1.pdf; http://www.fara.
gov/docs/5609-Supplemental-Statement-20060328-2.pdf;
http://www.fara.gov/docs/5609-Supplemental-Statement-20060929-
3.pdf; http://www.fara.gov/docs/5609-Supplemental-Statement-
20070323-4.pdf; http://www.fara.gov/docs/5609-Supplemental-

Statement-20070920-5.pdf; http://www.fara.gov/docs/5609-Supplemental-Statement-20080327-6.pdf; and http://www.fara.gov/docs/5609-Supplemental-Statement-20080923-7.pdf.

[56] See: http://www.fara.gov/docs/5609-Supplemental-Statement-20040829-I5KUBS02.pdf; http://www.fara.gov/docs/5609-Supplemental-Statement-20050228-IEH7IP04.pdf; http://www.fara.gov/docs/5609-Supplemental-Statement-20050930-1.pdf; http://www.fara.gov/docs/5609-Supplemental-Statement-20060328-2.pdf; http://www.fara.gov/docs/5609-Supplemental-Statement-20060929-3.pdf; http://www.fara.gov/docs/5609-Supplemental-Statement-20070323-4.pdf; http://www.fara.gov/docs/5609-Supplemental-Statement-20070920-5.pdf; http://www.fara.gov/docs/5609-Supplemental-Statement-20080327-6.pdf; and http://www.fara.gov/docs/5609-Supplemental-Statement-20080923-7.pdf.

[57] See: http://www.fara.gov/docs/5609-Supplemental-Statement-20040829-I5KUBS02.pdf; http://www.fara.gov/docs/5609-Supplemental-Statement-20050228-IEH7IP04.pdf; http://www.fara.gov/docs/5609-Supplemental-Statement-20050930-1.pdf; http://www.fara.gov/docs/5609-Supplemental-Statement-20060328-2.pdf; http://www.fara.gov/docs/5609-Supplemental-Statement-20060929-3.pdf; http://www.fara.gov/docs/5609-Supplemental-Statement-20070323-4.pdf; http://www.fara.gov/docs/5609-Supplemental-Statement-20070920-5.pdf; http://www.fara.gov/docs/5609-Supplemental-Statement-20080327-6.pdf; and http://www.fara.gov/docs/5609-Supplemental-Statement-20080923-7.pdf.

[58] See: http://www.fara.gov/docs/5609-Supplemental-Statement-20040829-I5KUBS02.pdf; http://www.fara.gov/docs/5609-Supplemental-Statement-20050228-IEH7IP04.pdf; http://www.fara.gov/docs/5609-Supplemental-Statement-20050930-1.pdf; http://www.fara.gov/docs/5609-Supplemental-Statement-20060328-2.pdf; http://www.fara.gov/docs/5609-Supplemental-Statement-20060929-3.pdf; http://www.fara.gov/docs/5609-Supplemental-Statement-20070323-4.pdf; http://www.fara.gov/docs/5609-Supplemental-Statement-20070920-5.pdf; http://www.fara.gov/docs/5609-

Supplemental- Statement-20080327-6.pdf; and http://www.fara.gov/
docs/5609-Supplemental-Statement-20080923-7.pdf.

59 See: http://www.fara.gov/docs/5609-Supplemental-Statement-
20040829-I5KUBS02.pdf; http://www.fara.gov/docs/5609-
Supplemental-Statement-20050228-IEH7IP04.pdf; http://www.fara.gov/
docs/5609-Supplemental-Statement-20050930-1.pdf; http://www.fara.
gov/docs/5609-Supplemental-Statement-20060328-2.pdf; http://www.
fara.gov/docs/5609-Supplemental-Statement-20060929-3.pdf;
http://www.fara.gov/docs/5609-Supplemental Statement-20070323-
4.pdf; http://www.fara.gov/docs/5609-Supplemental-Statement-
20070920-5.pdf; http://www.fara.gov/docs/5609-Supplemental-
Statement-20080327-6.pdf; and http://www.fara.gov/docs/5609-
Supplemental-Statement-20080923-7.pdf.

60 See: http://peacecast.us/2006/10/lisa-sullivan-on-the-us-torture-
school.html.

61 See: http://www.fara.gov/docs/5609-Supplemental-Statement-
20040829-I5KUBS02.pdf; http://www.fara.gov/docs/5609-
Supplemental-Statement-20050228-IEH7IP04.pdf; http://www.fara.gov/
docs/5609-Supplemental-Statement-20050930-1.pdf; http://www.fara.
gov/docs/5609-Supplemental-Statement-20060328-2.pdf;
http://www.fara.gov/docs/5609 Supplemental-Statement-20060929-
3.pdf; http://www.fara.gov/docs/5609-Supplemental-Statement-
20070323-4.pdf; http://www.fara.gov/docs/5609-Supplemental-
Statement-20070920-5.pdf; http://www.fara.gov/docs/5609-
Supplemental-Statement-20080327-6.pdf; and http://www.fara.gov/docs/
5609-Supplemental-Statement-20080923-7.pdf.

62 The information is all available here: http://www.fara.gov/docs/5609-
Supplemental-Statement-20040829-I5KUBS02.pdf; http://www.fara.gov/
docs/5609-Supplemental-Statement-20050228-IEH7IP04.pdf;
http://www.fara.gov/docs/5609-Supplemental-Statement-20050930-
1.pdf; http://www.fara.gov/docs/5609-Supplemental-Statement-
20060328-2.pdf; http://www.fara.gov/docs/5609-Supplemental-
Statement-20060929-3.pdf; http://www.fara.gov/docs/5609-
Supplemental-Statement-20070323-4.pdf; http://www.fara.gov/docs/

5609-Supplemental-Statement-20070920-5.pdf; http://www.fara.gov/
docs/5609-Supplemental-Statement-20080327-6.pdf; and http://www.
fara.gov/docs/5609-Supplemental-Statement-20080923-7.pdf.

63 See: http://www.fara.gov/docs/5609-Supplemental-Statement-
20040829-I5KUBS02.pdf; http://www.fara.gov/docs/5609-
Supplemental-Statement-20050228-IEH7IP04.pdf; http://www.fara.gov/
docs/5609-Supplemental-Statement-20050930-1.pdf; http://www.fara.
gov/docs/5609-Supplemental-Statement-20060328-2.pdf; http://www.
fara.gov/docs/5609-Supplemental-Statement-20060929-3.pdf;
http://www.fara.gov/docs/5609-Supplemental-Statement-20070323-
4.pdf; http://www.fara.gov/docs/5609-Supplemental-Statement-
20070920-5.pdf; http://www.fara.gov/docs/5609-Supplemental-
Statement-20080327-6.pdf; and http://www.fara.gov/docs/5609-
Supplemental-Statement-20080923-7.pdf.

64 See: http://www.fara.gov/docs/5609-Supplemental-Statement-
20040829-I5KUBS02.pdf; http://www.fara.gov/docs/5609-
Supplemental-Statement-20050228-IEH7IP04.pdf; http://www.fara.gov/
docs/5609-Supplemental-Statement-20050930-1.pdf; http://www.fara.
gov/docs/5609-Supplemental-Statement-20060328-2.pdf;
http://www.fara.gov/docs/5609-Supplemental-Statement-20060929-
3.pdf; http://www.fara.gov/docs/5609-Supplemental-Statement-
20070323-4.pdf; http://www.fara.gov/docs/5609-Supplemental-
Statement-20070920-5.pdf; http://www.fara.gov/docs/5609-
Supplemental-Statement-20080327-6.pdf; and http://www.fara.gov/
docs/5609-Supplemental-Statement-20080923-7.pdf.

65 See: http://www.usdoj.gov/criminal/fara/.

INDEX

175